Additional praise for
Peace, Butter & Jelly : Tales of Nourishment

Peace, Butter & Jelly : Tales of Nourishment is a gem with many facets. You realize after a number of pages that you have been invited to share food with the family of a masterful cook. In a profound and subtle way, author David Mark Seidel unveils the secret ingredient behind every successful recipe as he experienced it, as it nurtured and transformed him.

Like a great meal, the book is delicious, heartwarming, surprising and leaves you fuller than when you started. It is a cook book written by a poet, an honest sharing of a spiritual journey, and something more. By the time you finish this book, you realize that you were invited to dinner with great love and what was shared were recipes of the heart.

Roman Oleh Yaworsky, author, *Being Centered*

Reading *Peace, Butter & Jelly* is like having an easy and pleasant conversation with your own self, allowing you to reconnect to times of pure being. Gratitude reveals itself in each line, and it is contagious!

In this warm and inviting legacy that David has written for his son, David's heart pours out through every word, every line and every breath. This is a spiritual romantic's look at his own life through light, yet deeply profound, humor. Magic rests between the lines, where great meanings hide or reveal themselves.

Susana Sorí, artist, writer and healer

We applaud the work David is doing. *Peace, Butter & Jelly* will be a welcome addition to any food / family loving enthusiast's library. Very nice!

Gary Torres, Food For Life Baking Co., Inc.

Peace Butter & Jelly

Peace, Butter & Jelly

Tales of Nourishment

by David Mark Seidel

David Mark Seidel
Seidel Family Services, Inc.

Peace, Butter & Jelly
Copyright © 2011 by David Mark Seidel
All rights reserved. Printed in the United States of America.
No part of this book may be used or reproduced in any manner whatsoever
without written permission except in the case of brief quotations
embodied in critical articles and reviews.
For information address Seidel Family Services, Inc.
2301 Wensley Drive, Charlotte, NC 28210
davidmarkseidel.com

Edited by Judy Lynn
Designed by Latitude 35
Cover Photographs by Sarah Shoemaker Roberts

Library of Congress Control Number: 2011910294

ISBN: 978-0615504155

Printed in the United States of America

I dream.
That's all I do.
That's how I breathe.
That's how I am.

INVOCATION

I received the gift of a lifetime, meditation, on March 23, 1982. Meditation has unlocked my heart and allowed me to experience the magnificence of our existence. I wrote *Peace, Butter & Jelly: Tales of Nourishment* to share that gift, to share love.

DAVID SEIDEL
Ambition: To help bring peace to our country **Favorite Expression:** Ribet! **Favorite Memory:** Rock concerts at the Fillmore; Evening sessions on Cannon **Activities:** National Honor Society, Cannon Sports Editor, Treasurer of Interact Club, Student Council, Publicity Chairman of Debating Club, Ski Club, Marching and Concert Bands, Dance Band, Class Congress, French Club.

CONTENTS

Prologue	14
PEACE - The Tales	20
BUTTER - The Recipes	51
JELLY - The Poems	68
Epilogue	117
Dessert	120
Acknowledgements	125
Index of Recipes	127
Index of Poems	128
About the Author	129

DEDICATION

for Jeanette

She is light before light is even known
Water for thirst before it is even tasted
A step forward without even a glance either way
A breath always shared
She is forever knowing ways to free this world from pain
She is caring for everything and everyone and fully in all ways
I know her as my wife, as a place of God in my heart
which is the biggest, the strongest, the most dedicated;
I squeeze God tight just above the waist.

PROLOGUE

What is Peace, Butter & Jelly?

This book is for my son Jonathan and his planet, a legacy. I received an amazing gift, meditation. I am nourished by the practice of meditation, filled to overflowing. I want to give that extra to him and to others. I want to feed them well with stories, food and poems. A rich legacy goes forth to my son, a legacy that will stay with him and nourish him for years to come.

We live in a world dominated by devices, where life moves forward so quickly that any attempt at remembering, at legacy, is immediately eclipsed by the next move of our cursor or touch of our fingertip to the screen. Where did our family history go while we were building a life of electronic connections? What message will our children remember? The next one? The next one? The next one?

Or will we pause, decline our devices for a moment, look into another person's eyes and listen intently? Many of the people who shaped me are long gone; however, their remarkable stories define my daily existence. Without question, we are the product of legacies; and those people cheer us on. This book visits love, heartache, delight, craziness and exquisite wonder. These tales celebrate good folks: family, friends, teachers, the people I fed, and the person next to me in the check-out line. I want to remember their voices. Legacy matters.

We are short stories in the pull of the net. It's a swift planet. Adjust.

Take in the tales that follow in the next three sections: Peace, Butter and Jelly. Whether they are stories, recipes, poems or shenanigans, remember the three-part menu:

Peace is the foundation of our existence. Peace is harmony. Without Peace, our lives are more precarious. Peace is deep, from the inside out. Peace is our birthright. Peace is what allows us to hug a tree, and plant a new one after a devastating fire. Peace is remarkable. Hold on to Peace. Pause. Know Peace. Taste it. There must be Peace to get to Butter and Jelly.

Butter is so rich. Butter is a deluge of rain. Butter is good mileage. Butter is why we eat. We want to be fed and we want it to taste good. Butter tastes good. Sometimes we are out of butter; we forgot to buy it or somebody got margarine, instead. In that case, you enter the dreamscape of all culinary crusaders and exclaim, "I wish I had some butter for the broccoli tonight."

> Butter and the absence of butter,
> the passionate embrace and the half-a-handshake,
> sustenance and good fortune
> as well as lean times and gazing at the shelves when we cannot buy.

Never forget Butter. With Butter, we feel enriched.

Jelly is why you are smiling right now. Jelly is kids, 9 year old boys telling jokes about body parts that soon might grow, or what they heard on the playground. Jelly is a celebration of sweetness and the attempt at sweetness. Jelly is the excitement of the next meal, of what you think you might order if your grandparents take you out to dinner again to Bob's Italian Restaurant in Garfield, New Jersey. Jelly makes life fun even when it's hard, when the computer is acting slow or the cable guy still hasn't come or called. Jelly is not routine, Jelly is out of this world. Jelly

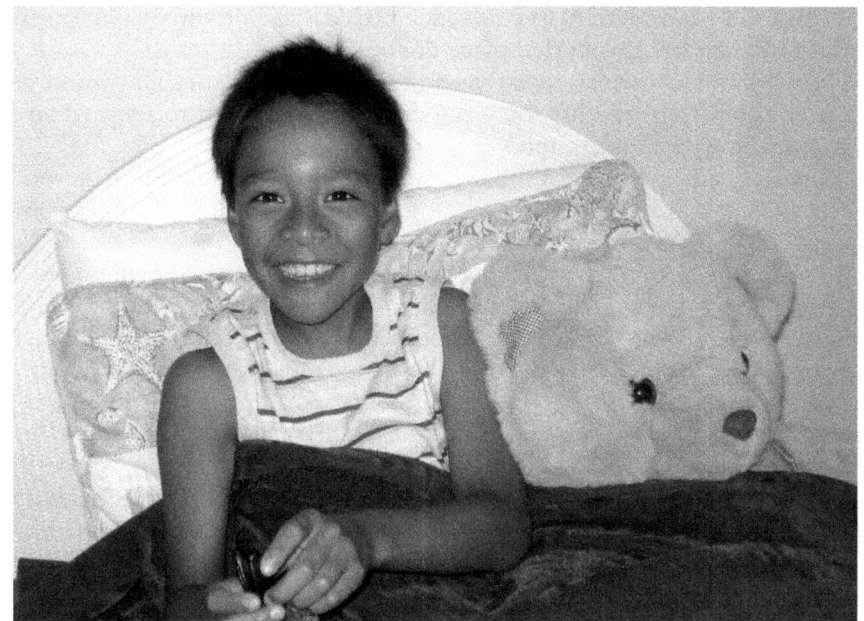

This book is for my son

is Ellington, Miles, Bird, and Monk. If you've never heard of any of these music masters, go out and buy yourself a record player right now and log on to Jelly, as in Jazz, as in America, and stay up all night and listen till all the Chinese take-out joints have to close. Jelly is a new day.

Peace is what makes the Butter sing. Jelly is the joy that follows. Follow the steps.

It's a good idea to read each Tale of Nourishment more than once. Initially, we read a poem to give ourselves permission to be the reader of it. As we read it a second time, we read the poem and the poem reads us back. The poem can show us its mystery and/or simplicity, and let us in.

I have sprinkled some extra condiments in the tales to encourage you to fall in love with the words. For the first time, you will use a collection of recipes written in kitchenease, the official culinary language of Peace, Butter & Jelly. Kitchenease allows the individual to enter a kitchen for the first time and make great food. Perhaps this is your first apartment, or your first marriage, or you are alone after decades of raising kids and you've heard a lot on the news about nutrition and wellness, then kitchenease is the language for you. How can you make food your friend? How can you make time your friend? With kitchenease, you stand before the counter, remember to breathe, and love all of life's ingredients. Gusto. Flavor. Purpose. You can cook.

We begin my family's story with my Grandfather. We called him Pop, his name was Barnet Seidel. He lived in two places, Russia and Brooklyn, and they are related. He told me this true tale when I was a boy, and my father reminded me of it. My heritage includes the smell of pickled herring on the kitchen counter next to the fresh-squeezed orange juice on a Sunday morning. Pop had an accent, all my Grandparents had accents; they all spoke a lot and I listened. I can see Pop's face, the long hairs that spiked his ear lobes, the size of his head, his physical carriage and a chest full of strength. How he made breakfast is still the deal in our home today. His kitchen was the storied place of nourishment.

My grandfather was enslaved at the end of the 19th Century. One hundred ten years later, I am a free man. My son is ten this year and I will turn sixty. When I was ten, this is what Pop spoke to me.

"I, Barnet Seidel, was born into a Jewish family of nine children, seven boys and two girls. We lived in Postaf, a small town in Czarist Russia; the area is now Lithuania.

We were very poor. The town was small. We had no factories where we could earn some money. We did have bazaars where the peasants brought their produce to sell. My father used to make a few kopeks by buying or selling farm animals.

Saturday, the Sabbath, was the only day we ate meat. Mother used to buy a calf head, as that was the best she could afford. On Yom Kippur, our holiest of holy days, we had the opportunity to bless a rooster (if a man) or a hen (if a woman) and partake of it. The evening before the fast of Yom Kippur began, we ate half of the fowl, and the following evening, after completing the fast, we feasted on the remaining half. That was the only time during the year that we ate chicken.

When I was five years old, my father wrapped me in the tallith, the sacred prayer shawl of the Jewish faith, and took me to cheder, the traditional seat of learning for young Jewish boys. For five years I learned to pray in Yiddish, the native tongue of Eastern-European Jews, and became fully learned in the Torah, the highest teachings of the faith. When I was ten, I was on my own and quickly moved away from town to seek a living.

My brother worked as a busboy in the region, so I sought his help. He got a job for me, also as a busboy. I had to get up at four in the morning to polish the guest's boots and feed their horses. My first two days I got up on time, then I overslept. The employer asked me why I didn't get up? He threw a three cent challah at me, and sent me away without any pay. (Challah is the traditional Sabbath sweet bread.)

I went back to my brother crying that I had lost my job. Meanwhile, a man arrived in the town looking for someone to apprentice in basketry. Word was sent to my father of the offer and the men agreed that I would work for three years, at twenty rubles a year. Furthermore, my father was required to submit a security of one hundred rubles. If I didn't last out the term, the man would take away my father's house. I gave my commitment, and my father sent a note of one hundred rubles.

To reach the basketman's town we traveled on horse and wagon all night. The man had a large house on a river. With a pull-over raft, one could transport a pair of horses and a wagon. I remember I was thirteen years old at the time, and often it was necessary for me to pull over the raft.

My daily apprentice duties begin first thing in the morning with the preparation of the samovar for tea. Breakfast was always tea with some bread. Soon after, the boss's wife would send me out to pick schav for the soup. (Schav is a wild green that makes delicious borscht.) One morning, I was so sleepy that I fell asleep in the ravine, and the entire household staff was sent to look for me.

To learn the basketry trade, I was set to work on a wooden bench eight feet long and four feet wide, with one end four inches lower than the other. I slept on the same bench, with a bunch of willows under my head. At four o'clock each morning I had to get up to start the day. At eleven in the evening I was finished. On Sunday, I had to get up just as early as on the other days.

For lunch, there were two herrings for three workers and three children, and also some soup with milk. In the evening we ate sour milk with bread. Everybody scooped food from one deep dish. There was not enough for everyone.

Life was nearly impossible when winter came. I found a place to sleep behind the stove, only big enough to sit in. For fun and to mock my warm place, the other workers took my shoe, scooped some water and threw it on me.

Conditions at the basketry continued to be unbearable. I wrote to my brother to come and take me away, but I received no answer. I had the keys to the closet where the boss kept all of his important papers. I stole my security note and hid it in the garret under the rafters. I wrote my brother a second time to please come and remove me from this place. Again, he did not answer.

Within five days, the boss went to his closet seeking some other documents and discovered that my papers were missing. He demanded that I return the missing papers. For three days I clung to the hope that my brother might come for me, but, again, he did not. The boss threatened that he would find the county sheriff and haul me off to jail, 150 miles away. He reminded me that 'jail' meant going from village to village, with each village council beating me. I was so scared. I could not return home to my father's house because there were small children there and very little food. Finally, I gave the papers back to the man and he laid me across his knee and beat me with his powerful hands. Finished, he stood up, then told me to go back to my bench and continue working.

I completed my apprenticeship and learned the trade in three years. For several years after that, I was employed as a Master Basketmaker, with a pay of two rubles a week.

As a Master Basketmaker, I was always involved in the fight to overthrow the Czar. I was viciously pursued by the Czarist police for my rebellious activities. Our group of revolutionaries received leaflets from Lenin in Switzerland. I would ride the rails to pick them up at our regional headquarters. When I returned to our town, I would throw the 35 pound bundles off the train so as to avoid the police at the station. I would then jump off and gather the bundles where they fell and hurry them back to my house. I used to hide the literature in metal cans under the manure in my father's stable. We shared these messages with the peasants who courageously seized the lands that had been ruthlessly managed by the local landowners and the Czar for centuries. As a result, our people finally had a chance to grow enough food to feed themselves. If an injustice was done, we corrected it when we could. Before I left Russia, we established the first library in our town with money we raised from the sale of crops and timber harvested in newly liberated land parcels and forests. I gave three years for a good humanitarian cause.

I sought greater peace and freedom in the United States soon after. Your father, Leo Seidel, my first child, was born in 1914 in Brooklyn, New York. We had a paint store in the Bushwick section where this photograph was taken. Your Dad must have been about 3 years old."

Pop and Baby Leo, Bushwick, Brooklyn

My grandfather would pause, recount again, sometimes in song, his journey to freedom in the city of Brooklyn. There was always a song from the old country that told of the struggle.

In 1951, I joined the family and the message of peace and freedom for all mankind was still ringing in my grandfather's voice. He never let up. And he held the Bushwick photograph to his heart as he sang.

Yes, my grandfather was enslaved. I am a free man. What did he live so that I could live? Was his hardship my gladship? I reflect on his tale and weigh mine:

1964 was a quieter time. Many fewer choices.
A three-way bulb in the living room
was a very big deal. Seat belts in our '57 Chevy?
They must have been made by hand,
and only one set sold. It was a quieter time.

God was mentioned, but I had no idea what I thought
I was understanding. We had hardwood floors,
and my parent's room had the only wall-to-wall.
When the week finished on Friday, it was really the weekend.
And when I lay under the covers on Sunday night,
I was ready to see how long it would take
for Monday homeroom not to come.

I was ready, my parents made sure of that.
God helped them to pay for the house.
I slept in that peaceful mortgage, while they strived.
I was happy and tired, and God was making me grow.

Pop shares a tale with David, 1971, Union NJ

PEACE

The Tales

Peace is for the planet. Jonathan's planet. I have traveled extensively and lived in many communities: Brussels, Brookline, Boulder, Bethlehem, Bombay, and Baltimore; all of which are in my breath, my bones, and the lasts of my shoes. My grandparents came by freighter to Ellis Island, New York. They were very young men and women, my mother's mother was 12 years old. They fed me. They sat with me at the kitchen table, which was covered with a yellow plastic cloth. They gave me extra bread and more soup, and a dollar bill before I left.

I love you Grandma Bess

God put my Grandma on the boat to America
at the age of 12.
She arrived at Ellis Island, said she was 16 years old,
and they believed her. When I met her 40 years later,
she had already received the first American patent in liquid nutrition.
It was called Soup of the Chicken
on the official certificate.
The name she liked best for her invention was
"Have-sum soup",
so that's what we called it. Dear Lord, a bowl by any other name
would never smell so sweet. I love you Grandma Bess, I'm so glad
He sent you over.

When I sat at her table, facing the golden glow of the clear broth and the gentle turn of the singular matzoh ball, I would pause. I would relish the peace that had been delivered to my place setting. I was about to eat the finest, most divine liquid a child could consume. My lips were ready for the warmth of silver, and my nose detected the scent of Grandma next to me, as she closely directed the wide bowl to its landing. Yes, it was liquid love, and there was serenity in my warm belly. Grandma stepped back to the stove, her altar, bathed in the 40 watt light of the range hood. Peace, my Grandma, a saint with a spoon; always offering more, always pretending like she didn't hear my response of "no thank you", making sure that I was content, that my life held no hardship or lack, that the magic of kitchen dexterity would always keep my life on course, and that I would feel happy, fed and full. Peace was not a dream for me as a boy. Peace was my tongue, my taste buds, my eyes, and my seat. Grandma's spoon and ladle had powers; they were enlivened. She fed her people. She was the conversation. Her recipe was goodness, some sorrow, and even sly jokes about the butcher who really liked her and scaled some extra on her recent order. I was in food love with Grandma.

I remember the contrast between each set of grandparents. Sixty-five years after Pop left home at the age of ten in Russia, I was a ten-year old seated in a box seat at Yankee Stadium for the World Series with my Grandpa Frank. My mother's father, Frank Saltz, loved baseball and we often watched games together. On that day, Mickey Mantle hit a home run in the ninth inning to win the game for the Yankees, 2-1. That same year Grandpa Frank took me to Aqueduct Raceway to watch him win big as the great thoroughbred, Carry Back, prepped for the Kentucky Derby. When Grandpa Frank purchased a new Cadillac Sedan De Ville each and every year, I was astonished. He took me to the car wash where the men would say, "Your Grandpa has so much money he could buy you a battleship!" as they shined and shined all that Cadillac chrome.

Grandpa Frank relaxing at his home in Passaic, NJ

I was raised in a Jewish home in Union, New Jersey, eighteen miles from New York's Times Square. An Hassidic Rabbi from Brooklyn commuted to NJ twice weekly to teach the Bar Mitzvah lessons to me. My friends and I loved the music and the chants we learned in afterschool Hebrew classes. I wanted more. I wanted a revelation or a new recipe that would transform what I ate and what I lived into a life that leapt beyond the stories of my family. Was it poetry, was it food, or was it music that would change my life and give me joy?

With graduation from high school imminent in 1969, the question of the day was: "What is my ambition?" Over 500,000 American men and women were serving in the Vietnam War. I was "serving" in high school and being called into the principal's office for wearing jeans, although they were dry cleaned and pressed. My response was published in our school yearbook: My ambition is to help bring peace to our country.

Two months later I was celebrating "Peace and Music" with 500,000 young people gathered at Woodstock. Three weeks after that I began my college education, finally free of high school foolishness. I pursued a college education that would both educate me and bring about social change in a school where everyone could thrive. Livingston College was a new campus of Rutgers, The State University of New Jersey.

We were the first freshman class, and our mission was simple: all races, creeds and colors could attend; we were there to learn; we had co-ed dorms; there would be no grades, only pass-fail-honors. It was a bold new day for higher education and we were seeking an extraordinary result: educated young people who would change the world and remove the darkness of the Nixon years. I sent only one college application; I wanted to join that great new beginning, an experiment.

David with his brother, Richard, at the Rainbow Room, NYC. College days.

When I completed Livingston in December of 1973, I had developed an exquisite passion for food and for being in the restaurant business. The family message that was imprinted at each meal was always about a more just and peaceful world, a constant striving as individuals to help create a better world. Perhaps we young people might redeem the struggles of our parents and grandparents and bring about a better quality of life. For me, born to taste and create with gusto, food became a vehicle to share wellness, wonder and secret sensations of culinary magic.

I traveled Interstate 95 north to Boston to seek the finest restaurant in New England and become a Professional Chef in the winter of 1974. As with my college choice, I had a goal to find the best place to learn, work and thrive.

I successfully trained and worked at Restaurant Maison Robert in Boston's Old City Hall Building, a classic European kitchen. When I left, I was ready to launch my own creation, the very first Personal Chef service in the City of Boston. Although it seemed as if everyone I spoke to wanted to have their own restaurant, I wanted to deliver restaurant quality food to people in their homes! I launched: "Open Your Own Restaurant Tonight...At Home!"

The Personal Chef business took off immediately, and was a success for both the client and me. Never before in Boston had a chef collaborated with families to provide them with a weeks worth of meals, ready to serve when they arrived home. Customers were thrilled.

When you develop a new concept in the food business, the rewards can be outstanding and occur quickly. Boston's largest department stores, Filene's and Jordan Marsh, immediately hired me to provide live in-store demos of my brand-new approach to family meal times. The local NBC-TV affiliate welcomed me to their "Good Morning" show which was broadcast to a large audience in New England and showcased the wonders of Boston's first Personal Chef. I was a very lucky individual, and I was about to experience greater good fortune by following my life's compass in a new direction.

Boston chef and amigo, Juan Rosa, welcomes David to the Dominican Republic

I was introduced to an opportunity to "dream big and dare to fail," a favorite quote from author Norman Vaughn. I had visited the Caribbean several times and was smitten with the peace and beauty of the Dominican Republic. That was where and how I recognized the place and lifestyle I wanted to live. But did I have the courage to choose a better world for myself? My family reminded me, "you were doing so well in Boston!" I was afraid and excited. Would my soon-to-be wife, Jeanette, agree to join me in the adventure? Two young people who had been dear friends for 10 years decided to develop a life together far from home.

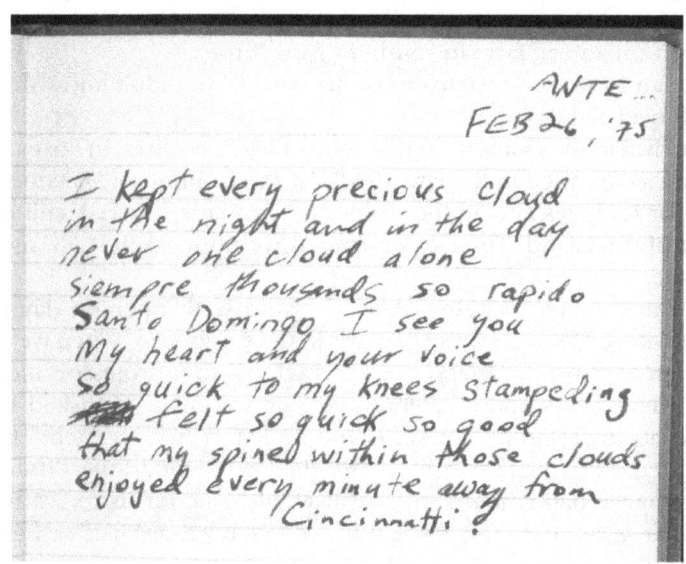

Rosa family on David's first visit to the Dominican Republic

Exactly one year after we were married, my wife and I left our successful careers in New England. She had been a bilingual, psychiatric-social worker at Boston's Children's Hospital, and I had been Boston's first Personal Chef. We settled in the Dominican Republic, a beautiful Caribbean nation, hoping to find peace and tranquility.

My wife is a child of the Holocaust. Her Mother was placed on the last Children's Train out of Berlin. Her Dad fled Vienna on foot with his father to seek safe passage to South America. His mother smuggled a diamond ring in a tube of toothpaste to their internment camp in Switzerland. My wife's parents later met in Caracas, Venezuela, were married and journeyed to New York City; they raised their children on an egg farm in southern New Jersey.

Jeanette and I were now citizens of the world. We didn't know that we would soon live all over the globe.

Upon arrival in the Dominican Republic in 1980, we lived in Sosua. This Jewish community was founded in the late 1930's by the Dominican Dictator Trujillo as a safe haven for refugees fleeing the Holocaust. Sosua is a sacred, still place on the north coast of the island. The day we landed we both asked, "Oh, my God, what have we done?"

Jeanette and I met in 1969 when we were both opening day pioneers of Livingston College. We were now pioneers in the Caribbean. When we called home after a few months on the island, we reached out to a professor, mentor, friend from our college years and a celebrant at our wedding. We asked him, "Lloyd, why did we do this? Go live on an island and start from scratch?" He chuckled and responded, "You were curious," and then he smiled long distance. We still wondered why we had come, and what it would take for us to last in this town. "Wouldn't it be great to live on an island?" How many times had we heard that one back in Boston.

We were living on an island in the sun. We grew this dream with steady results.

Our special love of food and friendship took us deeper into the hospitality business. We created a new destination in the world of travel, Casa Naima, Guesthouses and Villas on the Atlantic North Coast.

We began with an intimate bed and breakfast operation, then opened the island's first natural foods restaurant, followed closely by the first tour and travel agency, car rental and property management service. We were glad at business. We were the first to welcome the world to an unknown tourist destination, which today serves as the gateway to one of the leading wind-surfing beaches on the planet.

I did not recognize that imbedded in my dream of living on an island was a deeper longing. I can vouchsafe I did not even own the word "longing" at that time. My experience of so much beauty and tropical perfection was daily matched with the constant message, "I take my mind with me wherever I go". We had created the perfect life. We were the first local business to open when tourists began to arrive at our destination. I was sure that we were up to some amazing success. My mind was racing with ideas, while the village around me moved at the pace of an ox-cart or burro. I was filled with ambition in a land where one masterful dictator had once held all the ambition of a nation unto himself, while his people remained poor. I could go swimming every day among the coral and the schools of frisky kids, or tigeritos, ready to sell me soda and sundries every time I reached for my beach towel. When I wanted a smoothie, a member of our house staff would venture into the backyard, choose a ripe papaya, and I was good to go. I had people to make smoothies for me, sweep my front walk, and make my bed? Was it that good? Had I arrived at the success I longed for after leaving Boston blizzards far behind? I was seated on the most beautiful private beach in the Caribbean, but unable to make friends with my own mind. Peace? What about peace of mind? Peace of mind was not the active ingredient in the Ban de Soleil sunscreen I daily applied. It only took the visit of one man from the isle of Manhattan to introduce me to meditation.

Peace found us in Sosua in 1982, this peace was deep and forever. The visitor to Casa Naima brought his love of yoga and meditation to share, and we were ready. We meditated every morning without fail, from the first. In yoga, we call this an awakening of the meditative energy, a transmission of the meditative energy from the meditation master to the student. In our case, our teacher was in India, we were in the Caribbean, and the visitor from NYC was sharing his love of the practice. The visitor was the channel through which the force traveled. We were the lucky recipients of our teacher's clear intention to be fully present witihin us and make us new. The power of meditation was awakened inside of us, long distance.

The yoga scriptures indicate that a single look, word or thought from a master can transform a person forever. The transmission I received can not be measured with the noblest of scientific instruments. When I repeated the mantra of our teacher, I felt as if he had breathed his life force into me and transformed me through sound. I heard and felt a sound within my body that surged from the base of my spine to the crown of my head, where it rang a tone as big as the fire drill bell in junior high school. This unique moment was the turning point in my life. I entered a still place inside that was brand new, and at the same time I was certain this feeling of rapture was real. When the meditation completed, I stepped outside to view my world as if for the first time. Was that my street? Was that my palm tree leaning over the fence into Mrs. Biller's yard? Will you look at that sunset?

The ancient scriptures of yoga confirm that the experience of 'meeting' a master is rare. Those scriptures state that our first good fortune is to be born into a human form, instead of possibly a goat or a caterpillar form. The second achievement is that we can do self-inquiry as human beings. We can ask ourselves, why am I here? What is the meaning of life? The luckiest of lucky happenings is to meet a spiritual master and be guided to a relationship, a bonding, with the Universal energy which some call God and some call Spirit. The scriptures acknowledge this divine gift of Grace. I am certain that my life time is not big enough to hold all that I received on that day in 1982.

I discovered that God resides in my own heart, and for the first time in my life I was happy. Our hotel and restaurant business flourished, and I was an avid student of yoga. Sosua was a perfect place to meet God and make friends with my mind. My journey as yogi, meditator and teacher was ignited, and has endured for decades.

The result of this encounter with the mantra changed my life forever. The exquisite peace I had been seeking on the outside on a Caribbean island was pulsating inside of me. Meditation transformed my success in the hospitality industry into a starring role as me, David Mark Seidel. I was made worthwhile. I felt happy, and could use the word 'happy' freely in my communication. I was a meditator, a daily meditator.

David and Jeanette home from the Caribbean

Starting in 1982, we visited the Yoga center in the Northeast each year to connect to the teachings and the joy. The attraction of ashram life was supreme. We were living in the most beautiful beach community in the Caribbean, and we found something even better. Beauty was manifest in the ashram.

It was not an occasional experience of 3-D special effects at the movies, or an extreme mountain ski slope ride. We were the show and the lovers of the show.

We were so high from the daily practices of chanting, meditation, and service in the ashram that we were filled to overflowing. Each time that we arrived home to Sosua in the Dominican Republic, we had our full sights on the return to our 'spiritual' home in the States. "What do you want to do now?" our friends and family asked. They persisted: "Why would you guys want to leave such a beautiful place?" Well, we did.

Clear and complete in the Dominican Republic, we closed our business in 1985 to continue our studies of yoga and meditation. I gave our next door neighbor the trombone that I had played since junior high school. Jeanette gifted her yellow Schwinn racer to a big family that had worked for us. They would all gladly share the two wheels and the ten speeds. We took all of our recipes with us and sang our Yoga chants across the tarmac as we headed for Nueva York.

We left the island to consider living in the meditation ashram. It was by no means a done deal, however, we knew beyond the shadow of an incense stick that that we wanted to live there. Once back at my parent's place, our island belongings safely secured at the U-STORE-IT, it was time for the elders to speak their truth. My father put down his cutlery, slammed his fist on the maple butcher block table and spoke, "If you go to live there, I am never coming to visit you."

Leo and Jeanette

As a fellow yoga student remarked to us when we arrived in the upstate NY mountains, "So you gave up paradise to come to heaven?" Soon after arriving in the ashram, we were invited to remain as full-time ashram residents and staff members. I was glad beyond glad. We landed in the States on September 29, and one month later we moved in.

Jeanette and David, Catskill Mountains, NY

The ashram is an abode of peace where you can receive grace. We were called 'home'. We thought the Caribbean experience was a bold move. Now we embraced a unique destiny. Our family and friends had many questions. They still do. Ashram life is a spiritual practice. It is rigorous. It is distinct. It's not for everybody. People missed us a lot. We understood, and we were steadfast in our resolve to choose the sacred as our lifestyle.

David and Jeanette in Goa, India

Every visit I made to the ashram meditation temple reminded me of two things. I helped to build that temple, a holy place for seekers from every corner of the earth. In addition, I owe my life to the individual who changed my heart forever. I owe my existence to my teacher and the lineage of meditation masters who have catapulted me through this life. With their grace and blessings, I offer this book and its contents. I would never have met you on these pages without the gift of yoga, without the guidance of a living spiritual master.

The ashram, a beautiful retreat site, is an easy drive from my parents' home in New Jersey. Two weeks after we unpacked, my father and mother made the first of many visits. For more than nine years, including three years of intensive training in India, we were immersed in the teaching and practice of yoga. We taught people about the benefits of yoga and meditation in Canada, South America, India and over 60 cities in the United States. After a single one-week visit to the Charlotte meditation center during those years of touring, I told my wife that one day I would like to live in a place like Charlotte. After 14 years of living a dedicated 'retreat' lifestyle all over the world, my wife and I chose to start a family and settle in the Carolinas. Our ashram experience was complete, for now.

It was time to move out and see what movies and television had been shown in our absence. Tom Hanks and Jerry Seinfeld were not visible in our Sanskrit vocabulary. To this day, I have never visited an episode of the show. I am sorry, Jerry, your program was eclipsed during that time. We grew to love all of Tom's movies, especially Forrest Gump, written close to our own lives' timeline.

I remember the shock when we visited Walmart our very first time, even before the Supercenter was born. Standing in the toilet tissue aisle, we felt confounded and estranged from the consumer experience. Were we visitors from Mars or gringo shoppers fresh from the womb of cloistered life? We were dazed. We felt silly, like Proctor and Gamble had put us in that aisle so that they could laugh at us. We squeezed all the valuepacks envisioning them watching on hidden cameras in the corporate office in Cincinnati.

Packed and ready to move to Charlotte

The transition from ashram life to Charlotte, North Carolina continues to define our lives today. In America, post traumatic stress syndrome occupies our attention daily as we soften our presence in distant conflicts and return our troops to their neighborhoods and familiar surroundings. The dream state is a vast arena of deep memory and needed healing. We did not experience stresses in the ashram, we lived blessings there; we were the lucky guys. The separation from the womb of protection the ashram affords left us feeling a deep loss for the lifestyle and dedication permeating that community. To this day, I experience my dreams almost every night as focused on the ashram, as if I never left my spiritual family; and/or I am en route to India, trying to connect me and my bags at the terminal half-way in Franfurt, Germany. Both the experience of war and the experience of human kindness, love and respect create lasting impressions. How we spend our lives, the company we keep and the actions we perform imprint our cells with a picture that is forever percolating in our psyche. As much as we wanted to leave the ashram to become house-holders, the ashram would not leave our hearts.

I had to come up with a resume to capture the work experience that defined those years of dedicated service and devotion. What kind of resume would I deliver to my first prospective employer? I heard the title, God is My Resume. I can write a book about my experience of God in everything and in everyone. Somehow, I will evoke the same mood in a brilliant resume format. This resume evolved into my own small business, eventually more than one business venture. Some of the heart of that book, God is My Resume, appears in these pages ten years later.

Five years after leaving the ashram we purchased our first home, and our newest domestic scene emerged.

> Each time my wife cleans the house,
> she vacuums behind all the outlet covers.
> Yes, she takes them off, runs the baby Hoover,
> and puts them back on.
> When we take a shower, she insists we dry the tiles with a cloth to
> prevent build-up when we're all finished.
> She places the orange sack on the curb each month for the Vets.
> Old clothes.
> One time she pulled my silk topcoat from the bag,
> made an inside vest pocket button perfect,
> just in time for the orange truck 8:30 AM deadline.
> She loves our new home.
> She places God on every mantel, facing each appliance
> and down in the grout of the master family bath.
> The first split-level temple in the world.
> "We're unpacked. Come worship with us soon in the Carolinas!"

We came to Charlotte to start a family. We had lived a modern monastic life in the ashram for more than nine years. As my wife frequently describes me, "David loves to meditate, he loves to cook, he loves to write, he loves to love his family, he loves to create new businesses, he loves to see if we can create an ideal world. David's goal is a heart connection."

Now it was time to grow our marriage into a family. After losing a pregnancy to miscarriage, we were about to give up:

The deep peace of breakfast before the news.
Oh, what could happen, anyway?
There hasn't been a new script in years.
Except, people are busy like mad.
For some, rest never comes.
One continuous cappuccino, scalding hot and portable.
Electronically, the connections seem brilliant.
Face to face, the skin is dull, and the whole outfit is
of a color that never met the sun.
I, too, am alive in this moment of racing forward,
except, I meet a friend in the juice aisle,
commerce waits, we can talk,
the apricots and elderberries listen within their crystal chambers:

>   She lost a job.
>   We lost a child.
>   We hug, we are thankful again.

I shop for serenity. Deep pockets of peace.

    It was time to try the adoption route. We were nearly 50 years old. We dug in. After a failed domestic adoption when the agency went out of business and kept our five thousand dollars, we hardly knew how to keep going. We embarked on the international adoption journey.
    At the height of it, I wrote:

>   The perfect amount of words.
>   The perfect way to say them.
>   Nothing is disregarded, every sound is essential.
>   We want to be parents, have a family, of course it happens
>   all the time all around us.
>   Look at any parking lot near any store and there you have it:
>   People are together and with kids and they are somewhat unified
>   in their purpose and probably did not consider at all any factors.
>   We consider all.
>   We adopt a life. We receive another breathing being as our own kin,
>   deeply related in an instant of powerful dreadful waiting,
>   a long drawn-out ordeal of legalness that takes our strength and reduces
>   it to whining and collapse.
>
>   We love Love. What else is the point?
>   Please God, our lives
>   a true son
>   of God.
>   Bless that child.

Jeanette holds Jonathan for the first time

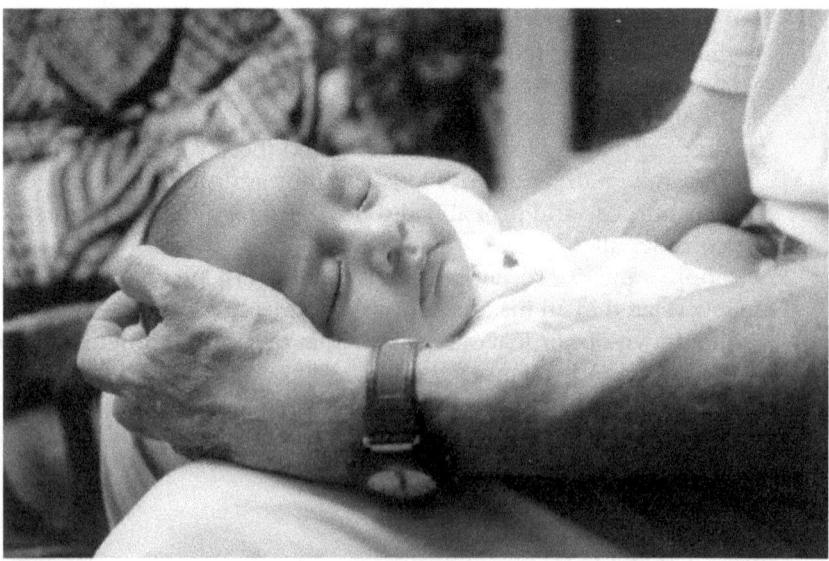

David cradles Jonathan for the first time

We adopted our son, Jonathan Domingo, in Guatemala City the week of September 11, 2001. We arrived in Guatemala on September 6, 2001 with tickets booked through World Trade Center Travel in New York City. When the US Embassy re-opened on September 13, ours was the first adoption to process; and ours was the first flight when the airport re-opened on September 16. Peace? What Peace? Our son was four months old when he left his birth country to join our country, starting in North Carolina.

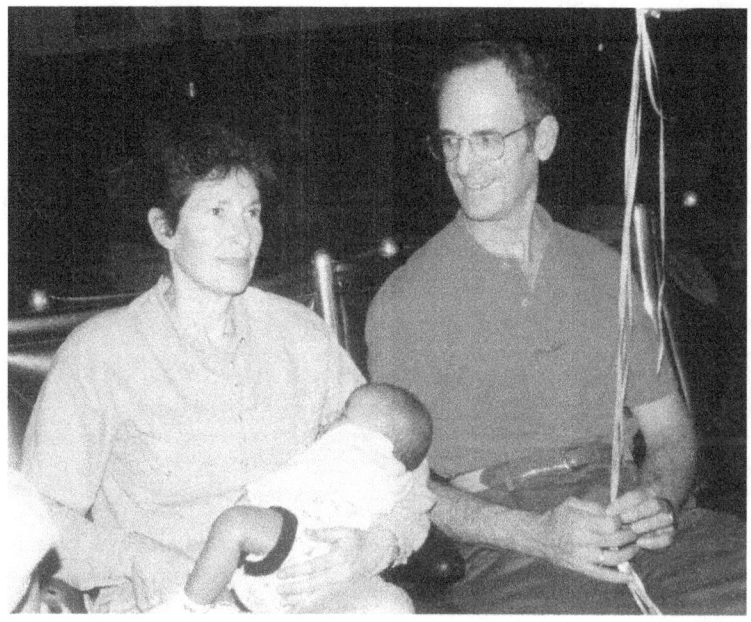

Jeanette, David and baby Jonathan arriving home in Charlotte.

As I wrote him, some years later:

> We are a family, a funny family.
> 55 years ago our country bombed
> the country where you were born.
> You weren't born yet.
> Yes, that is what really happened,
> what will you remember?

How much Peace can we feel in a lifetime? In Sanskrit, the word for Peace is Shantih. Shantih is the "Peace that surpasseth understanding". Shalom, the Hebrew word, means "Peace be with you". In Arabic, the word is Salaam. The full stroke of Peace covers the planet. What if we let there be Peace?

I can sing this tale each morning to my son as I walk him to the bus stop:

> Across the street.
> Around the block.
> Over there…

35

The driveway poet says:
There's something that the earth does,
as a planet.   It turns.
Now, we see daylight.
Now, we shift.
                       (it's your turn.)

Jonathan waiting for his first school bus ride

    Butter. Butter is for abundance, lots of it. Spread it all around. Organic Butter, not If It's Butter, or Lite Butter, or Carefree Butter, or Whipped Butter, or Butter Flavor; we want Real Butter, the kind the cows in Vermont intended. We also want pastries, sauces, cookies, peach cobbler, bread, and bread and butter. My mother says her two favorite foods are bread and apples, but she also loves butter on her bread. When I travel home to visit with her, I bring bread; she loves the gift, whether its cinnamon raisin or scones or sprouted, she is ready to eat.

Dear Mom, Florence Seidel

When she picked me up after school, as a boy, we would stop at the corner store and purchase a fresh loaf of Jewish rye. The man sliced it and placed the contents in a brown paper bag, no plastic, no twisty.

> Mr. Sommerman had a grocery store. He had canned goods and a deli case, with fresh potato salad and carrot-beet coleslaw. He made them himself. He wrapped bologna behind his back, told my mother she looked great, and gave me a salted pretzel stick, unbroken, all at the same time. Standing in the sawdust up to my laces, I would ask the other pretzels in the tin, 'What other God is there than a big man, half-apron, half-glass?'

The trip back to the house was less than a mile. Together we ate half the loaf, with nothing on it. What a treat we shared!

I created my first recipe using the rye loaf. It was a sunny Saturday morning and Mom had gone to the A&P to purchase the weekly groceries. She said that if I got hungry I could make myself a sandwich, with whatever was in the refrigerator. She had not returned by 12:30 and I was starved. In the cheese drawer was a package of A&P swiss cheese, individually sliced, a very hefty cut per slice. Alongside the cheese was a previously opened can of Hershey's chocolate syrup, covered with aluminum foil to maintain freshness, since we only used it for birthday parties. I was ready to eat. I grabbed two major slices of rye, placed them on the bread board, removed the foil from the syrup, and carefully selected the last two pieces of swiss. I considered: cheese first, or syrup first, on the bread? I opted for chocolate first and poured a decent amount over each slice. Slowly, I arranged a slice of cheese on each side of chocolatey bread and closed the sandwich securely. Too hungry to get a plate or even sit down at the kitchen table, I raised the creation to my lips. The first bite sent the syrup out through the holes in the rye bread covering my fingers and sleeves. Was it the cheese or the chocolate? Nobody was going to eat this combination, and how was I going to get rid of it before my mother came home? David's first recipe included three ingredients: awful, unforgettable and nine years old.

David at Washington School

As I tell my brother, we learned around the kitchen table. That's where all the teachings were given, and where my father made sure we understood our responsibilities to our fellow human beings. Dad ate very fast. When he spoke, we listened. When he shared that we should treat all people the same and that we are all equal, my Mom's Milani 1890 Corn Flake Chicken was the perfect food for such a noble man. My Dad was a provider. A view of our home movie might look much like this:

> My father never dried his legs after he took a shower. He only used a hand towel, so that was as far as it would reach. When he ate tuna it was straight from the can. The same with sardines. In winter, when it was freezing cold, his gloves stayed in his pockets, they laughed in there, while he shoveled huge amounts of solid snow. His whole life he loved people, he hugged them like mortar to a brick. He knew God, but never mentioned the name. My Dad filled me to the bone: *David, my boy, I love you - have fun, keep well - best of everything. Dad.*

Leo and Florence

My family, the people who brought me to this page, still have questions about my exact livelihood. They clothed me in McGregor sport shirts and Stride Rite shoes, they watched me grow six feet tall, and most of all they spoke to me. They shared stories and information about everything I could possibly understand. I was curious and they fed me tons of stuff. We learned in our house, and that was love. It was the love of learning, knowing more and hearing the latest WOR Radio news. We didn't have a tablecloth at breakfast. All my father had to do was open The New York Times and it covered half the kitchen. I had terrific grandparents who gave me money every visit, sang to me with gusto like Caruso, squeezed my freckled cheeks like they were jaw breakers, and fed me a diet direct from God in Heaven. Everything was delicious, and I could always have more.

Grandma Bess, my mother's Mom, was my heart's delight.

As summer baked the streets of Passaic, New Jersey, Grandma Bess wondered why my brother and I needed to play guns in "such a heat", with our corduroys and leather shoes and "get so overheated." Meanwhile, she was preparing two Breyer's ice cream cups on the stove in a gentle bath of warm water in her favorite sauce pan. She would step to the door and usher us inside to get out of the heat and into the paper cups, half vanilla, half chocolate, about to melt, not too cold for the system. Grandma was the best part of every day. If you asked her spirit now why her grandson played forever with guns and later wrote a book about peace, her response surely would be, "Go figure… I should know?" Then she would turn back to the stove and ask you, "you want some challah with your chicken? I can toast you some."

David and Richard Seidel

Leo directs the cowboys

Grandma, I have been a vegetarian for 30 years. My son has never eaten a hamburger. I would love for you to cook for us tonight. We can use your golden tablecloth.

> This is the vegetable hour. Years have passed since liver and swiss steak.
> Carrots tell onions tell beets tell me the difference.
> I'm so healthy I must look like a model for Forever Magazine.
> I'm worth a fortune and most of it's roots and minerals.
> I pray, and I eat, and my satisfaction could fill the continent.
> Glory to God, and every potato, each kernel of corn, all the rice can cover.
> This is the vegetable hour before dessert!

Grandma was the best part of every day

I have prepared and served food for four-plus decades, and everything I've ever done has been eaten. I love to cook. I was born to make things taste great. I began with Cream O' Wheat Cereal, and then added Toasted Kretschmer Wheat Germ. I developed the neighborhood tuna casserole for my college roommates, baked every muffin recipe variation in *The Joy of Cooking*, pledged my full allegiance to the mission of *Diet For A Small Planet*, and dropped fries and grilled sandwiches at The Tides Diner in Beach Haven, New Jersey until one day I entered the kitchen doors of Restaurant Maison Robert in Boston. Chef Jean Paul hired me to wash butter lettuce, prepare baby shallot vinaigrette and create thirteen yolk crème caramel. I became a chef because I was always dreaming of flavor and gathering ingredients. I love to cook. Here, try this. You will find me in your belly. Nourishment is my legacy.

> The word is Love.
> Constant Love.
> No fluctuation. Peopled with splendor.
>
> I will gift you a divine soup,
> a golden bowl of nectar.
>
> Who says not to slurp with your spoon?
> You may slurp all.

I write daily. I meditate every morning and when the meditation completes I have my pen ready with my journal. I must write. As a student of mine shared about her meditation, "In my life, it is like exercise and flossing…necessary for overall health and I don't feel right when I don't get to it."

Is writing a form of meditation for me? Yes. I also love to write about writing, what the pen does, how the paper feels, if there is enough light in the room. And then I feel full.

> I will colonize your mind with poetry.
> Mostly short stuff,
> Many brave words.
>
> Do you still read ink?
> Hey, how's your penmanship?
> There must be something
> you'd like to dream today?
>
> Don't tell me I'm lying
> when I say your work is so special.
> Go ahead, pick up the pen.
> You're a writer, like me.
>
> Spread out,
> Use both sides,
> Tell your story.

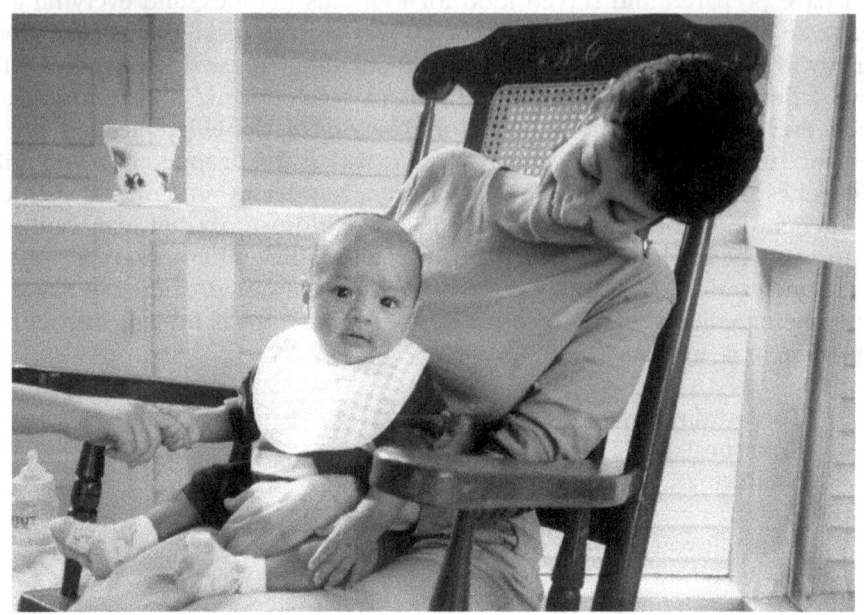

Jeanette rocking Jonathan on our porch

Mommy tickles Jonathan

Jonathan's first summer

Jelly is for the Joy. I am a father, a husband, a friend. And if I'm really lucky, I might get to share the joy of writing this book with you. When I began in January of 2010, it sounded like this to my on-line readers:

> In this new year, I hope to reach out to you
> on a daily basis with a few words to bring us closer
> to joy, closer to our hearts, closer to what it is we
> are feeling on a daily basis. The emotional soup?
> A spiritual weather report? A lot of nonsense?!
>
> Perhaps, at the end of the day we can make
> a big pile of Thank You Notes and share them with
> our friends.
>
> I include you as a way of thanking you for being in my life.
>
> Good night for now, see you in the morning!

I called the collection "Thank You Notes 2010". Today you read me as *Peace, Butter & Jelly: Tales of Nourishment*.

> Yes, I did it all. I went into the world.
> Yes, there are a thousand fishermen.
> I stayed,
> that was all it took.

When my wife and I landed in Charlotte seventeen years ago from the ashram, we didn't have a chair, a dishtowel or a rake. Today we have an insinkerator, window treatments, a three-legged cat, a four-legged cat, and a ten year old boy, our very own son. What is it like to become a father at fifty? Would I call the next book, The Brutal and the Bliss? Is it painful to repeat yourself so many times a day about a task as simple as brushing your teeth? Some days, yes.

> All the other families in pressed white linen are lining up neatly at the sand dunes for the perfect sunset photo shoot.

David loves his boy

Jonathan can come up to me ten times a day and exclaim with full clarity, "Daddy, I love you." I used the words 'I love you' on my wedding day. I was twenty-nine years old and that was the first time for me.

As Jonathan and I listen to Car Talk together on the car radio, he understands the abiding principle of life that Click N' Clack espouse, "Hey, we're just makin' it up!"

> Make believe I lived today:
> I did this day for the life of me,
> I gave congratulations.
>
> What's it like to live with Jelly in my life?
> I will go into his room this evening, after he has fallen fast asleep,
> and place my lips on the crest of his chocolate cheek bone and kiss him.
> How does it feel to be the guardian of so much beauty, fire and youth?
> He will be young forever it seems,
> but will you, his Daddy?
> his Mommy?
> his friend?

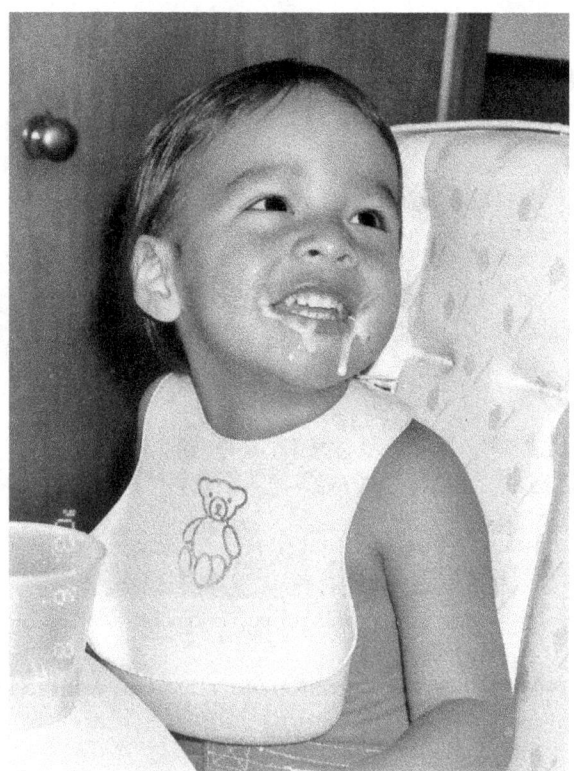

Jonathan loves Stoneyfield

Hey! Look at Peter Cottontail
Hoppin' down the bunny trail -
Now, that's a way to start the day!

Are you hungry to begin?
Are you a morning person,
Is that what you're good at?

Peter looks for carrots.
We reach for the phone
to see who called last night.

Our legacy is not a digital one.
As you rub noses, what you touch
comes home.
We have all kinds of friends
   in the garden,
We have all kinds of pets.

Mama bear and her cub in our garden

Jelly is for the Joy. Jelly is for North Carolina. Do you want to know what a nice place North Carolina is to live? This story took place an hour from our home.

> She was born in 1935.
> They named her Delight after the way they felt that day.
> Her brother's name was Safety.
> They lived in Polkton, a small North Carolina mill town,
> where the product, the only product, was piano bench seat cushions.
> Safety was the plant manager, Delight designed all the fabric.
> We sit on one, now. It's held up real well for its age.
> How old is God? How long has God been making things
> in little North Carolina towns?
> Can God remember everything God's done?
> We thank God,
> We thank Delight,
> We thank Safety,
> and we thank those people who keep things going.

Jelly is for the sunlight. We get plenty of that in North Carolina. Jelly is for the rain, "falling down on plants parched to sticks," in the words of a great poet saint. We experience the effects of global warming in Mecklenberg County, North Carolina:

> We need rain so badly
> the earth would give anything to be the sky.
> God is even considering looking for other work.

Look at Daddy!

Jelly is for the soup, any time of the day. There are no compartments in my family legacy that are separate from soup. My mother's soup is a constant in our household. It must be served so hot that the spoon ignites when it reaches for the broth.

>There were things in my mother's soup
>I did not understand.
>Vegetables and meat pieces you cooked,
>but never, never ate.
>They lay on the counter, before the water boiled.
>They floated in the pot
>no matter how much she stirred.
>They were unusual and irreplaceable.
>They had to be used or it wasn't soup.
>Mom's secret recipes hold unspeakable treasures.
>Today we call the vegetables organic,
>we worship them as original foods,
>and we fry them in good oil as a snack.
>Our complete history of health is in the soup.

Here is a list of 33 cities in which I made soup for my students and friends. This journal entry covers a period from 1986-1989. A geographical review of where the joy was served, where the soup was supped:

May 10, 1988 (Cape Cod)

Remembering as I walk the Cape, all of
the places I have walked these days,
these years,
in Buenos Aires,
in Miami, in Tucson,
in Tallahassee, in Charlotte, in Montreal,
in Boston, in Rio, in Denver,
in Austin, in Dallas, in Redding,
in Seattle, in Quebec, in New Orleans,
in San Diego, in Chicago, in Ogallala,
in Eugene, in Mendocino, in Tahoe,
in Albuquerque, in D.C., in Vancouver,
in Phoenix, in Atlanta, in Ft. Walton,
in Davenport, in Charleston, in Savannah,
in Scarsdale, in Amherst, in Albany.
I am in all of you, everywhere.

David and Jeanette complete a meditation teaching tour at Lake Tahoe, California

In all the classes I taught and business I conducted, the keystone of the relationship with my student, client or reader was, "What's it like to be you?" I continue to want to know, "who are you?" Can you tell me more? Can you be specific? What is the stuff you are made of?

What if we had fun and made something together that tasted good. We could serve it at our gathering or hold it for ourselves. Are you hungry to know, or are you just hungry? What kind of concoction would you like to make? Do you cook? What is your best recipe?

This recipe was handed down by telephone from Long Island to New Jersey in 1961. It had just snowed a ton, and my Mom was going to treat us to our favorite winter 'stew'. Her friend Sylvia recommended it, and that meant it had to be delicious. Sylvia and Mom called it The Concoction. My brother and I would fight over who got more and who got to lick the saucepan. We were sturdy folks in 1961 and nobody asked questions such as, "What's it like to be you?" The only self-inquiry Sylvia offered with the recipe was, "Did I get it from Thelma or did I get it from Rose?" Sylvia never paused to listen inside for her answer. When you tasted it, you knew that these ladies were the best cooks around!

THE CONCOCTION

1 can Campbell's Cream of Mushroom Soup (10 oz.)
1 can Chicken O' the Sea Tuna (5 oz.), drained
1 can Green Giant Le Seur Peas (8.5oz.)
1 hard-boiled egg, chopped
1 med. baked potato, cooked, small dice
Put all ingredients in a small saucepan, heat,
Stir often, and serve very, very warm.

At Mom's table

**I dream.
That's all I do.
That's how I breathe.
That's how I am.**

David and Jonathan on family retreat

BUTTER
The Recipes

Our Caribbean natural foods restaurant and bakery was christened La Cocina Magica, Spanish for The Magic Kitchen. We fed the tourists and the neighborhood with an assortment of from-scratch recipes that heralded a new day for eating delicious and celebrating local ingredients.

Many of those 'secret' Magic Kitchen recipes are shared in this text for the first time in print. One of those creations in particular, La Fanega, The Official Magic Kitchen Veggie-Burger, is a keeper. Its popularity was so keen that a hungry eater seeking his ultimate burger fix changed our CLOSED sign to OPEN one day by flipping the wooden shingle; he then entered the premises to insist on his meal. We were roused from our siesta, fired up our trusty Black and Decker Toaster Oven and ten minutes later Burger Man was on his way to the beach with his Fanega in hand.

The story of the sourcing of the ingredients for this meal as well as its name is a foodie's adventure supreme. So you want to open your own La Cocina Magica? This is what it took in 1982 to bring this blessed burger to market:

Inspired by reading the healthy-eating "bible", *Ten Talents*, I set out to create the ultimate veggie-burger with available ingredients. This meant finding whole grain brown rice, wheat germ, calabasa, the local squash/pumpkin known as auyama, whole soybeans, and bulgur wheat in a country in which most people primarily consumed four foods: plantain bananas, yucca root, rice and beans. We were about to dramatically shift the supply chain for a nation of millions. All of the foods necessary to distinguish La Fanega were already produced in our region. We happened upon the trail of goodies after following many distinct leads:

- Our local bakery produced a perfect 'pan de aqua' with the purest white flour from the mill 30 minutes away. We needed wheat germ, and the mill produced truckloads of the stuff which they sold to pig farms as a feed supplement. The mill owner, an Italian man who understood our request, produced a sack of wheat germ that would fill a 55 gallon drum. He charged us about three US dollars.
- The calabasa happened to grow on the mountain overlooking our town beach, an easy find, and happily provided by Farmer Felix. He had been selling it only to weekenders, visiting from the capital after a long journey. We then became his best local customer for years.
- The bulgur wheat was produced in the capital by Middle Eastern families, remembering their food heritage and selling to other lovers of their cuisine. The capital is over 5 hours drive from our restaurant.
- Thank God for the pigs, again, as we had the whole soybeans ready for them and the chickens, who needed soy in their feed products. Soybeans were locally grown and always available at the neighborhood bodega grocery/ farm supply depot.
- The whole grain brown rice must have come from the 'field of miracles' because all of the rice grown on the island, a nation of rice and bean eaters, was shipped directly to the mills to create the white variety. We were sent an hour from home to a small farm that was willing to sell us a sack of rice before it was placed on the truck for the mill. This precious sack of rice, weighed approximately 50-60 lbs. and was called Una Fanega of rice; it was a sack full of gold to us. Una Fanega was a pre-metric system measurement equivalent to a 1/4 bushel of grain in the USA. We chose the name La Fanega to honor

the treasure we had secured and the burger we created. Grain by grain, we cleaned the rice by hand, and the recipe was prepared.

LA FANEGA

> 1 ½ cups whole organic soybeans (soaked overnight in 4.5 cups water to cover)
> 1 cup red onions, course chopped
> 1 cup ripe tomatoes, course chopped
> 2 T fresh cilantro, course chopped
> 3 T lime juice
> ½ cup pumpkin seeds (from the calabasa)
> 5 T Bragg's Liquid Aminos
> pinch of ground cayenne
> 5 t sea salt
> ½ cup fresh coconut pulp, small chunks
> 5 T olive oil
> 2 cups soybean water from soaking

Blend all of the above, a little at a time, in a blender, food processor or Vita Mix.
Pre-heat oven to 350 degrees.
In a separate large mixing bowl, gently stir:
> 1 ½ cups grated calabasa pumpkin, peeled (medium grate)
>> butternut squash may be used if calabasa not available
>
> 1 cup organic bulgur wheat (soaked overnight in 1 cup soy water)
> 2 cups cooked organic brown rice
> 1 cup red peppers (sweet) diced fine
> ½ t oregano, dried
> ⅓ cup raw wheat germ
> ⅓ cup organic corn meal (as in cornbread)
> whole sesame seeds
> paprika

Add wet ingredients to dry and pour into 9x13x2 Pyrex dish oiled with 2 T olive oil. Raw mix is 2" deep. Extra amounts can be baked in smaller Pyrex squares or loaf pans at the same time.
Dust top of Fanega with wheat germ, whole sesame seeds and paprika before baking.
Bake at 350 degrees uncovered for 80 mins. Allow to cool for 15 minutes before slicing. Serve on a toasted Ezekiel 4:9® bun with a side of favorite coleslaw. After serving, freeze leftover portions as individually wrapped burgers.
YIELD: 12

You must be hungry, want a little something before reading more recipes? Cooking La Fanega makes you think about what you will serve for dessert.

The Rice Pudding Recipe is a great place to begin. Growing up in the land of New Jersey, the roadside diner was the mecca of Rice Pudding. The holiest of holies was on Route 1, just north of New Brunswick and next to Piscataway, NJ. This landmark establishment was The Edison Diner, known to the locals and the kids in my dorm as 'The Edison'. At any hour of the day or night, depending upon which cycle of the sun's rays we were observing and which stimulant was our motivation, a pilgrimage to The Edison was a royal feast for about 95 cents. Rice pudding was a forever food. It will always remain so in our house. Served warm, served cold, topped with Real Whipped Cream, sweetened with maple syrup, we are talking miles of Route 1 comfort in each serving.

RICE PUDDING COMFORT, Holiday Style

3 quarts organic whole milk or unsweetened soy milk
1 ½ cups white basmati rice (organic or imported from India)
8 T local honey (1/3 cup)
¾ cup organic unsalted butter (1.5 sticks)
1 ¼ t sea salt
2 t vanilla extract (fair trade, please)
5 cloves (with large heads, crush heads first)
¼ t cardamom powder, if available
¼ t ground nutmeg
4 twists of orange peel (navel or juice)
½ cup organic thompson seedless raisins

Combine all in stainless 6 quart pot and gently bring to a boil, stirring frequently for another 15 minutes. Allow to cool for 30 minutes before serving or cool completely and refrigerate. The completed pudding stores well in the refrigerator and makes great gifts. This quantity is a holiday portion. The recipe can easily be reduced for smaller gatherings.
Yield: 16

What will we have for dinner tonight? What about a wonderful soup and some quinoa pilaf? Since humankind lit the first fire to feed the first broth, we have enjoyed soup on every continent. People lean on soup for a good reason. It is easy to prepare, inexpensive, and darn healthy. I come from soup. My ancestors was soupsters, like rapsters or hipsters. Soup was their native tongue and means of exchange. As I learned to cook, the world taught me the bowl and cup language, soup was everywhere; someone knew how to make a homemade soup and taught me the secrets that stirred the pot.

I give you now the steady wisdom of kitchenease, the liquid language of soup. I play kitchenease on one instrument, the stainless steel pressure cooker. In our home, we prefer a 6 quart model. The size is perfect for batch cooking and freezing, fits easily on most stovetops, and washes up comfortably in the average sink. Can you prepare soup in a stock pot? Absolutely, go right ahead. You will need to adapt time and temperature (see instructions). The pressure cooker allows for maximum nutrition retained and much less time in the kitchen. Within 30 minutes, the pressure cooker will deliver a bountiful Miso Soup ready to serve. And, you will have leftovers for a few days, as well as some ready to freeze. Miso soup matched with an exotic quinoa pilaf, and you are in business!

MISO SOUP

4 carrots, chopped
1 medium onion, chopped
3 large cloves garlic, sliced
3 celery stalks, chopped
4 cups fresh kale, chopped, leaves and stems
1 T ginger, sliced
1 bay leaf
1 t sea salt
1 T olive oil
1 pkg. extra firm tofu, small cubed, about 30 pieces
3 quarts purified water, plus the tofu liquid, some vegetable stock (pot liquor) is even better than water! Watch your salt.
2 T organic sesame tahini
4 T miso paste, organic brown rice, aged 2 years, preferred

Place all ingredients except the Tahini and Miso in the 6 quart pressure cooker. Bring to full heat and let cooker rock gently for 15 minutes.
Using a 6 quart stockpot: Cook for at least 45 minutes at medium boil, well covered, then let stand.

Remove pressure cooker from stove and allow to cool in sink under tap water before opening.
Open lid of either style pot and ladle 1 cup of broth into a small mixing bowl containing the miso and tahini. With a dinner fork, stir the bowl until the solids are dissolved. Add this blend to the pot and continue heating another 5-10 minutes without pressure lid. Never allow the miso liquid to boil. Remove pot from heat carefully, stir, adjust seasoning for salt and add optional cayenne pepper to taste. A richer Miso flavor can be obtained by adding additional miso using the small mixing bowl method. Serve hot, never boiling, with the Exotic Quinoa Pilaf.
Yield: 10

About the Quinoa Pilaf, let's begin with the word 'Quinoa', pronounced Keynwah. Sourced from the ancients in South America, this wonder grain will transform culinary skills in less than 30 minutes. You may have served brown rice pilaf a million times, it is time to move on to Exotic Quinoa. The cooking time is half that of brown rice and the nutrition is formidable. Quinoa outranks any other whole grain as the most complete food we can eat. Begin with a smaller serving and notice how satiated you feel: such is the measure of the exquisite and exotic life force that is locked inside each tiny grain.

Talk about easy and you don't have time to cook, enter Quinoa, and soon you will have your own show on the local food network. Emerging young chefs know that Quinoa leftovers make great veggie burgers and super casseroles. Breakfast hounds swear by this grain as the secret of their morning ritual. As with all of the recipes in this book, you are comfortably guided through the language and execution of kitchenease; you will emerge a confident cook although it may be the first time you have fed yourself and/or your family. Look at that, you know how to make Exotic Quinoa and Miso Soup.

EXOTIC QUINOA PILAF

1 cup organic quinoa
2 cups purified water
1 T olive oil
pinch of sea salt
⅓ cup raw cashew halves
small bay leaf
clove of garlic, split, (optional)
½ t whole sesame seeds

Place grain in 2 quart saucepan. Rinse the Quinoa well with tap water and drain. Bring pot to stove and add all ingredients except sesame. Cook covered on medium heat until all liquid is absorbed (10-15 minutes.). Turn off heat. Never stir. Sprinkle sesame seeds to cover and let stand at least 10 min to allow grains to further expand. Fluff grains and nuts gently and serve. Multiply with ease for larger groups.
Yield: 4 – 5

David climbs Grandma's steps

Jewish food and Jewish cooking happen to be my ancestral taste bud. Noodle Kugel, or Noodle Pudding, is religious as in delicious. My parents taught me the mantra Kugel years before I learned to meditate or chant. Kugel is a special food, often reserved only for the New Year's meal, or the Sabbath, or the birth of a child. Make this recipe and enter the realm that gave the world bagels and chicken soup. Invite lots of friends. If you have the wish, make a double recipe as it freezes well. You can also partake of it for days from the refrigerator.

NOODLE KUGEL

1 pkg. egg noodles, 12 oz. (Manischewitz original whole egg)
3 T unsalted organic butter
4 extra-large eggs, beaten
2 cups whole milk ricotta cheese
¾ cup Stoneyfield Organic Whole Milk Yogurt
8 oz. pkg. Neufchatel Cream Cheese, softened at room temperature
3 favorite apples, peeled, cored and chopped in two inch chunks
1 t vanilla, fair trade please
2 t cinnamon powder
½ cup organic light cane sugar
1 t sea salt
organic brown cane sugar, for dusting
2 T fresh lime juice
½ cup thompson seedless raisins, soaked over night in water to cover

Preheat the oven to 375 degrees. Butter 9x13x2 Pyrex dish. Cook noodles in purified water with a pinch of salt, until almost done, al dente. Drain well. Place in Pyrex and mix in the butter. Let stand.
In a large mixing bowl, combine all ingredients, except apples and lime juice, and blend together with wooden spoon and rubber spatula. Pour mixture into Pyrex and cover with apples and lime juice. Dust with cinnamon, brown sugar and a sprinkle of salt.
Bake for 40 minutes until golden brown and well done. Cool slightly before serving.
Can be served slightly warm or at room temperature. Note, many teens consume kugel straight from the fridge. If left out before refrigerating, it may be consumed by the dish crew.
Yield: 8

Summer in the South is abundant fruit, to the point we can't stop eating vast quantities of the stuff throughout the day. The pause comes when the thought arises about 9:30 AM, "wouldn't it be great to have some of that peach and blueberry cobbler that we made for company last month?" The kitchen walls gleefully resound, "Why only for company? Can't we have some of that for our dinner tonight?" And sure enough, we have tons of ripe peaches ready to go, and the blueberries, there are extra pints stashed in the back of the fridge. Five months later as Winter Solstice nears, the urge returns again; thanks to the abundance of apples that drop in the Carolinas and the luscious blues we saved in the freezer, the recipe emerges again to welcome our friends that gather for Yule time and the like. Cobbler is always a hit. It's so easy and well loved. The house smells great for days as you re-heat it often. You can freeze a portion, however, you must be dreamin' about make-believe leftovers.

PEACH AND BLUEBERRY COBBLER

    2 cups blueberries, fresh or frozen
    3 cups very ripe peaches in season, sliced or chunks
    ⅔ cup organic light brown sugar
    ⅔ cup pure water
    4 t arrowroot powder

Slowly bring all the above to a boil in a 4 quart stainless pot. When fruit thickens somewhat, stir in:
    4 T unsalted butter
    3 t lime juice

Place fruit in Pyrex 9x13x2 baking dish. Let stand.
Pre-heat oven to 350 degrees.
For Crust, sift together:
    2 cups flour (organic unbleached white)
    3 t baking powder (Rumford)
    ½ cup organic light brown sugar
    ½ t sea salt
    cinnamon powder
    1 stick melted unsalted organic butter (¼ lb.)
    1 cup organic whole milk

Add wet to dry. Combine until smooth, but do not over beat. Drop topping in large spoonfuls over fruit and sprinkle with 2 T cinnamon powder or cinnamon sugar, if available
Bake at 350 for 20 - 25 minutes, until nicely browned.
Substitute apples in season for peaches and use 4 cups favorite apples (Rome, Pink Lady, Macintosh, mixed), peeled, cored and cut in two inch chunks. Let the kids help with this one. Lucky children.
Yield: 12

Enter something fresh, as we combine raw fruits and vegetables to create a refreshing smoothie called Morning Greens. We still eat granola, puffed grains and oatmeal, however, the world of raw foods and the energy they provide can eclipse the comforts of cooked foods and sweets. Drink a glass of this blended goodness and your clear mind will thank you as your body rejoices with lightness and ease. As you learn the recipe, you may adapt the ingredient balance to accommodate seasonal selections and climate. Soon, this type of product will be dispensed as you drive from your in-dash food center, programmed from an international culinary GPS to source the most local ingredients direct to you and your vehicle.

MORNING GREENS (Energy Soup)

    2 cups apples, cored, peeled (optional), cut-up
    4 cups greens (favorite sprouts, fresh spinach)
    1 T dulse (powdered seaweed), if available
    ½ cup juice (unsweetened pineapple or apple juice)
    ½ ripe avocado

Blend all in machine of choice, large blender, Vita Mix, or food processor
Serve immediately. Refrigerate no more than 1-2 days. Drink it with friends. Boy, is this stuff good! Kids will crave it for after-school, after-swim, after-homework refreshment.
Yield: 3 (8 oz.) servings

Here's an easy recipe at any hour of the day. In our house, it is the national anthem. So go ahead, throw some on!

BUTTER AND YEAST on CRUNCHY BREAD

Toast a few slices of your favorite crunchy bread. How about a crusty semolina or sourdough, Ezekiel 4:9® Sesame, or French Meadow Spelt? Generously apply organic unsalted butter to the slices and THEN, sprinkle the wonderful, magical, Large Flake Yellow Nutritional Yeast (Red Star brand) over the slices. With your knife, carefully mash the yeast into the buttery bread. You can top this delight with ripe avocado slices, banana or apple slices. See where your tastebuds go, as the combinations are endless. This is our son's all-time favorite snack. If you have no crunchy bread handy, than open some Lundberg Organic Rice Cakes and follow the above instructions. If you are a meat lover, be sure to try this spread; the savory flavor of the yeast flakes may remind you of a hefty smothered onion reduction on your favorite piece of lamb or veal.

    Our Magic Kitchen Restaurant opened in 1982 in the oceanfront community of Sosua on the North Coast of the Dominican Republic. The name derives from a well-heeled recipe that has fed thousands over the years, since the wonders of condensed milk and the practices of yoga and meditation came face to face. A Yogi may occasionally have a sweet craving after hours of meditation and chanting. The combination of coconut, chocolate chips, condensed milk, cookie dough and nuts is a great reward and a delicious friend. In our case, we had none of the ingredients available to the typical North American restaurant owner. Our recipe was fleshed from all the local resources we could muster, and at the end of the day, we had two amazing desserts, a name for our establishment, and a product line of double header sweets. As with La Fanega, the tale of how the Magic Squares were made would do Hogwarts graduates proud.

The foodstuffs grown locally in the Dominican Republic were lucrative export items. Before the sweet milk, peanuts, pure cocoa powder, coconuts and plaintain bananas from our neighborhood were taken to the seaport, we played interceptors and brokered small quantities to fill our stockroom. We created our own fine chocolate, gathered and grated the coconut to perfection, shelled and roasted the peanuts, and even scored the best condensed milk before Nestle shipped all their product to US ports. The platanos, or plantain bananas gracefully ripened to perfection in a dark corner of our open air porch. When all of this was ready for assembly we guaranteed our customers a dessert that transcended the sweetest tropical breeze or oceanfront vista.

Chocolate Magico is sweet, but the Fruta Magica is recognized as the epitome of fresh fruit combined with coconut, sugar and cream and then placed on a tender dough. The flavor of baked platano maduro, or fully ripened sweet plantain, rivals chocolate any day. Why? Imagine a fruit essence that merges banana, pineapple, mango, and apple with the abundance of sweet potato and calabasa pumpkin? Whether you are a student, parent, dreamer, happy eater or on vacation, remember La Cocina Magica and the legacy of real taste. Which Magico will you choose? I dare you to try both.

CHOCOLATE MAGICO / FRUTA MAGICA

Crust:
1 cup wheat germ, raw
2 cups organic unbleached white flour
1 ½ t sea salt
4 T local honey
½ cup organic whole milk
¼ cup canola oil
1 t vanilla extract, free trade please
¼ cup organic unsalted butter, melted

Pre-heat oven to 350 degrees.
Measure dry ingredients in mixing bowl, then add all wet items and stir until all blended. Do not over mix. Pat gently into bottom of 9x13x2 Pyrex bake pan. Bake six minutes until set. Allow to cool.

Chocolate filling and topping:
2 cups semi-sweet chocolate chips
1½ cups freshly grated coconut or can be fresh frozen and thawed
1 14 oz. can organic sweetened condensed milk
1 cup chopped nuts, walnuts, pecans, or peanuts, your choice

cinnamon powder, optional

Fruta filling:
4 cups ripe platanos, steamed soft, and mashed, approximately 7 platanos, ripe platanos are completely black and soft, even mushy
2 T fresh lime juice
1 t sea salt
⅛ t ground cloves
pinch of cardamom powder, if available
⅛ t cinnamon powder
¼ cup organic unsalted butter, ½ stick at room temperature
platano liquid from cooking

Fruta topping:
1 ½ cups freshly grated coconut
1 cup chopped nuts, pecans or peanuts
1 14 oz. can organic sweetened condensed milk

Assembly of Chocolate Magico: Slowly pour milk over entire crust. Layer gently with chips, coconut, and nuts. Now, mash it all into the crust with a fork. Dust with cinnamon, optional. Bake 35 minutes at 350 degrees until lightly browned. Cool thoroughly and cut-up into squares or triangles. Great for freezing in sealed container, w/layers of wax paper. Although it stores well at room temperature, it keeps longer in the refrigerator during hot days.
Yield: 24

Assembly of Fruta Magica: Pour and spread milk over crust. Hand mix all ingredients to create fruit filling in mixing bowl. Platano liquid may be added for ease of spreadability. Spread fruta filling over crust and cover with coconut and nuts. Remember to gently mash it down with a fork into the crust. Dust with cinnamon powder. Bake 35 minutes at 350 degrees until lightly browned. Cool thoroughly and cut-up into squares or triangles. Great for freezing in sealed container, with layers of wax paper. Again, this stores well at room temperature, though it keeps longer in the refrigerator during hot days.
Yield: 24

Do not argue over the merits of Chocolate Magico vs. Fruta Magica. You are standing under the same tree, looking out over the generous vista of the Atlantic. Spread your blanket and share your wealth. Take time deciding which one to try first. Remember, always share.

Breakfast. Breakfast in Bread, Breakfast in Bed, Breakfast around the world. Can I tell you how important it is for you to have a good breakfast each morning? We never missed breakfast in our house. There usually was a fight to get enough space at the table: with my father's fully spread New York Times and my brother and I positioning our cereal boxes, to prevent any sharing of the Chex Press on

Wheat Chex and Rice Chex cereal boxes, or the latest Kellogg's promotion for baseball heroes of the day. We ate a lot of the dry stuff (hot cereal was saved for special days) until one day my mother handed me the apron and said "sure, you can make your own Cream O' Wheat"; and young Chef David was born. My hand on the spoon assured me a lump-free morning cereal that was smooth and creamy. Oh, to see the butter melt on the surface before serving. Childhood happiness and emerging artistry, Golden Blossom honey and a dust of wheat germ came next. Good Morning Cereal was only a few years away!

Make your own cereal and see how much time you actually do have in the morning and how good you can feel, to boot. How did I learn to cook? Easy… in the morning!

GOOD MORNING CEREAL

½ cup organic quick oats
a few raisins, organic thompson seedless
1 cup pure water
pinch of salt

The night before, place contents in small saucepan to sit till morning (covered). You can program yourself to do this while you program your coffee maker. I am going to make this recipe so quick and easy for you. Rise and shine, while admiring the beautiful day out your window, add:

1 ½ cups organic whole milk or organic unsweetened soy milk
a little banana or apple, finely chopped
pinch of clove or nutmeg
a twist of orange or lime, if you'd like

Adjust liquid quantities for more or less milk to water.
Cook all until the pot thickens, about 6 minutes, with the lid partially open.
Yoga students, this is the perfect time to practice kitchen counter yoga or your favorite chant.
Forget the radio, the Web or your phone and dance around the kitchen. If you haven't done last night's dishes, then do that yoga while the cereal cooks.
Allow cereal to stand, covered another 5 minutes and dust generously with:

raw wheat germ
cinnamon powder
1 pat of organic unsalted butter, a little more if you'd like

Light a candle. Invoke the day, a Wednesday. "Lord, there is still a chance. I am a good person." My cereal says, 'Good Morning.' Easy to reheat the next day by adding milk. There are no Microwave ovens present in the Peace, Butter & Jelly kitchen.
Yield: 2-3, depending upon morning appetites

Take the book with you to work and tell your friends that you made your own breakfast this morning. Show them the recipe. This Friday you can do a morning cereal conference call and time each other. I have eaten this cold on campus or in the car many times and loved it, topped with Vanilla Stoneyfield Whole Milk Yogurt. Turn up the speaker phones at the stove!

Cake. Dessert. 9:30 in the morning. The author Anne Lamont, when asked by a Charlotte audience, "how do you start the day as a writer?" playfully responded with "I have dessert before I begin to write." This is the cake that Anne would bake, the Peace, Butter & Jelly Chocolate Cake. This is the cake you think of when you are having friends over for a birthday celebration. The flavor is wonderful, it's moist, chocolaty, and as easy to prepare as the muffin recipe you just clipped from Parade magazine. This particular recipe originated with carob powder as the main ingredient. For thousands of years, spiritual seekers have transitioned between carob, the fruit of the St. John's bread tree and chocolate, the fruit of the cacao plant. This recipe can go either way. Carob powder is a luxurious food taste and wonderfully nutritious, while chocolate imparts passion, stimulation and ecstasy. See what works for you. What will you treat yourself to at 9:30 A.M. this morning? Cake!

PEACE, BUTTER & JELLY CHOCOLATE CAKE

> 1 ⅔ cups organic unbleached flour
> 1 cup organic light sugar
> ½ cup organic unsweetened cocoa powder, fair trade please
> 1 t baking soda
> ½ t sea salt
> pinch of cardamom powder, about ⅛ t
> 2 cups Stoneyfield Organic Whole Milk Yogurt
> ¼ cup organic unsalted butter, melted
> ¼ cup canola oil, expeller pressed
> 1 ½ t vanilla extract, fair trade please
> 3 T organic thompson seedless raisins, soaked overnight in enough water to cover only, water is not for cake
> 3 T nuts, slivered almonds or pecan slices, nuts are optional

Preheat oven to 375 degrees. Butter and flour 8x8x2 Pyrex baking dish.
Sift together dry ingredients. Blend together wet ingredients by hand. Add wet to dry and stir until smooth. Pour batter into Pyrex (dust with nuts, if desired) and bake 30-35 minutes.
Yield: 8-10

Peace, Butter & Jelly Chocolate Cake partners beautifully with a scoop, or several scoops, of your favorite vanilla ice cream. Happy Birthday! Hey, why is everyone at the kid's table raising their hands?

Chocolate cake is an essential part of the human diet. Even if you never eat it, knowing of its whereabouts and wonderfulness helps the spirit. Chocolate helps us to grow and be better human beings.

Now, a triple toast to the best cornbread, the best casserole, the best pudding!

BEST CORNBREAD

With special appreciation to Susie Biener's Mom in Nashville, Tenn, who created the original taste template that got me started. The Magic Kitchen cornbread recipe began, formally, sometime in 1975. Since then, the recipe has been closely held. Now we can all enjoy some. Make sure you stick to the specific brands and ingredients, as there are no substitutes.

Dry:
3 ½ cups organic corn meal
½ cup organic unbleached flour
6 t Rumford Baking Powder
2 t sea salt
nutmeg, freshly grated, a few grains
sesame seeds, un-hulled, brown, nutty color

Wet:
3 cups organic whole milk,
1 cup Stoneyfield Organic Whole Milk Yogurt
2 T local honey
½ cup Spectrum Canola Oil, refined is ok

Assemble all ingredients as oven preheats to 425 degrees.
Apply 1 T of Canola Oil to entire 9x13x2 Pyrex interior with napkin or paper towel and preheat, while mixing wet and dry bowls separately.

Add wet to dry and mix swiftly with rubber spatula, but do not over mix. The batter can have some lumps. Remove hot oiled Pyrex from oven with mits and place on hotplate surface.
Pour the batter into the form. Steady the pan and level the batter with spatula gently. Sprinkle with sesame seeds. Carefully place Pyrex in center of hot oven. Bake time is approximately 20 minutes. Remove with care. Test with toothpick to ensure that center of bread is dry. The bread will sound hollow as you tap it if done. Remove cornbread to cool dry spot. After five minutes, take a stick of unsalted organic butter in hand and lather across the crust of the bread. Lightly coating is good and let your guests know that the butter is already on it.

If consumed within two days store in an air-tight container, in a cool place. It can be frozen immediately when fully cool, however it does tend to crumble a little after defrosting and then reheating in a gentle oven. No microwave, please. Yield: 12

Tortilla Mamita Casserole is healthy Mexican food filled with organic ingredients and resplendent with taste. This recipe premiered on WBT Radio's What's Cookin show in Charlotte. It is a custom-built concoction that can be easily manipulated when you have mastered casserole building. Put something in, take something out. Parents, they may not help you sweep the kitchen, but they will love this entrée and invite their friends to worship this creation well into the night.

TORTILLA MAMITA CASSEROLE

Create a delicious polenta lasagna filled with beans, rice, cheese, veggies and exotic Sprouted Wheat Tortillas from Alvarado St. Bakery. Equipment needed: 4-6 qt. saucepan, wooden spoon, chef's knife, cheese grater or slicer, 9x13x2 Pyrex baking dish, aluminum foil.

Ingredients:
4 cups organic whole milk
1 cup organic yellow grits
2 whole eggs
1 cup organic cooked kidney or black beans
3 whole tortillas, (Alvarado St. Bakery Sprouted Wheat), cut in quarters
1 ½ cups organic tomato sauce
1 cup organic cooked brown rice
½ cup Organic Stoneyfield Whole Milk Yogurt
1 cup grated organic monterey jack cheese
½ cup Organic Stoneyfield Sour Cream
¼ cup grated Italian cheeses (asiago, parmesan)
1 t sea salt in milk
crushed red pepper to taste
3 T olive oil
2 bay leaves
½ t cumin seed
1 t oregano leaf
½ cup organic carrots, chopped
½ cup organic celery, chopped
½ cup organic green onion, chopped
½ cup organic mushrooms, chopped
5 - 6 ripe medium tomatoes, sliced

Purchase and assemble all ingredients. Ask for a blessing and breathe. Pre-heat oven to 375 degrees. Heat milk in saucepan. Chop all veggies and add to milk. Add salt, pepper, olive oil and spices. When milk is ready to boil, gently stir in the grits and keep stirring. Cook grits till good n' stiff. Blend in grated parmesan or asiago cheese. Let stand covered. Beat 2 eggs. Grate or slice the jack cheese. Slice up tomatoes, if available.

We are now ready to assemble the 'Mamita'. Please note: the brown rice as well as the beans are cooked ahead, and can be from the night before. The beans, if necessary, can be canned.

Gently oil the baking dish with olive oil. Swiftly stir the two beaten eggs into the polenta mix.
Pour about ½ the mix into the dish and spread to cover the bottom. Spread a layer of yogurt, a layer of cheese, and a layer of tortilla pieces to mask the polenta. Paint all with sour cream and some of the tomato sauce. Pour more polenta and cover with brown rice, beans and sliced tomato. Salt lightly. Layer final pieces of tortillas, any remaining polenta, and top with tomato sauce, sour cream, and jack cheese. Dust with sesame seeds. Cover entire dish with foil and bake on middle rack for 50 minutes; breathe deeply, it's in.

Remove after 50 minutes. Remove foil and set it aside. Return dish to oven and bake uncovered about 10 minutes more, or until well-baked. Remove from oven and re-cover the dish. Let stand away from heat to cool. Serve after 30 minutes with a gorgeous green salad.

Portions of MAMITA can be frozen when cooled. To serve, please defrost in the fridge and reheat in an oven or toaster-oven at 350 degrees until ready. Never microwave food. MAMITA is also wonderful without re-heating, from the fridge. Or leave out at room temp for a few minutes, like a slice of quiche.
Yield: 8

And now with some pleasure I
find that its seven; and must
cook dinner. Haddock and
sausage meat. I think it is
true that one gains a certain
hold on sausage and haddock
by writing them down.

-Virginia Wolff

The folks who created Trader Joe's have been rightfully honored in this book, and for good reason. I love to shop at my neighborhood store because its fun, the people who work there love their job and the shelves are always happy. Open a bottle of your favorite white wine, the staff pick of the week, and get ready to celebrate Peace, Butter & Jelly. When it comes to kitchenease, Trader Joe's is the most advanced academy on the planet.

Food is a celebration. A simple bread pudding is easy and filled with a sense of wonder and accomplishment. You can combine the wet and dry ingredients and, bingo, you are the best baker in town!

TJ'S BEST BREAD PUDDING

Ingredients:
1 Trader Joe's Organic Spelt Bread, 20 ounce loaf, yields 8 cups cubed pieces
½ cup pecans, chopped coarse
6-7 extra large whole eggs, well beaten
½ cup organic raisins, soaked overnight in purified water, water not included with wet ingredients.
6 cups organic whole milk or organic unsweetened soy milk
⅓ cup organic cane sugar, light
4 t vanilla extract, fair trade, please
1-2 T fresh squeezed lime juice
1 t sea salt
6-7 apples, cored, peeled, sliced, can be jonagold, pink lady, or macintosh, fat slices preferred
Blend 1 t cinnamon, 1 T organic brown sugar and ½ cup chopped pecans for dusting the top

Assembly: Butter (unsalted) 9x13x2 Pyrex baking dish. Pre-heat oven to 350 degrees. Prep all dry ingredients. Prep all wet ingredients with sugar and salt. Place dry in Pyrex dish and cover with all wet. Dust with cinnamon/sugar/pecans, and sprinkle with lime juice. Bake uncovered until browned and happy, approximately 45 minutes. This pudding freezes well.
Yield: 10

JELLY
The Poems

A note of thanks.
I kept saying I would write to you,
                and I did.
I will not back-off a single word.
I graze the pen in the pulp of the page.
                Breakfast.

I don't have to pick a horse that everybody is going to like.

We need for the sun to shine.
We need for the stars to come out,
            and twinkle.

We need for our car to start.
We need for our kids to behave.

So, what do we want?
What is the measure of our satisfaction?
A plate of warm noodles and a crisp salad?
More time to meditate?
Who will fold the laundry, who will make the bed?

I know you've got to go, I want to say, "Good morning",

                    "You're welcome".

Today starts this way, in the reaching words.

The only technology that can serve the mind is meditation.
Imagine that? Nothing else works.
Nothing else can even get close.

Pause now, while you are young. Give your mind a rest.
Because if you don't begin now, a steady practice,
at some point old age arrives,
your body forces you to pause, you have no more leg power,
and there you sit,
an old person,
with a mind that never paused.

There will be no peace, days of it.
And what will you do?
The meditation class was years ago.

You don't have to read
somebody else's words.

Go ahead, write it down.

Write it down with a stinging pen
in a journal fresh from a Chicago bindery.

You are the language champion,
    not me.
Put me out of business now,
and write it all down.

Declare yourself.
Put it in writing.
Use fierce punctuation.

Own me through the words.

Everybody on the planet needs a break.

And the Lord went and opened the crust
                in the Caribbean.
Another interval of change,
        peopled with death and heartache.

So why am I smiling?
My friend lost his home and his family.
Is this a new day for Haiti?
or another day for Haiti?

There is so much I don't understand
about the winter salmon sky this morning.

And we have birds and we have trees
                          in the Carolinas.

Oh, how I wish we could put our earth back together.

Teaching, consulting,
completely rewriting the script of the world,
our civilization:

Who is this David guy?
and what does he inspire in others?
A presumptive. A world class presumptive
with the ultimate prescription for change.

Am I the poet who went to work?

I got the job!!

When I was finally hired last week
by the Department of Defense
as the Assistant Secretary of Interior Affairs,
They were delighted to know
that I had already navigated the human interior
as a meditator, on four continents.

The two year position,
to develop and implement a new brand/identity emblem
for the organization,
pays $250,000 per year.

Some possible choices so far are:
                Dept. of Sense
                      or
                The Sense Dept.

What is your preference?

All submissions are welcome.
If you have a feeling either way,
please let us know.

We will decide.

I have taken every chance in the book.
I have taken the book.

A hug for Daddy, the birthday boy

Into the wagon that carries her oxygen,
Beverly places her oak leaves,
one leaf at a time.
I pass her on the access road and I can remember
when she coached the girl's field hockey team in junior high.
She smoked in the teacher's room in those days
and looked like Donna Reed.

"If you can breathe, you can smoke,"
was probably the line she used if any of her star athletes would ask her
in health class. And then she would add, quickly,
"God knows why I do it."

Beverly and God have this arrangement
about her lungs and the wagon.
Today, a leaf picked up, put back,
for every butt she tossed in the teacher's parking lot leaving school.
As the wagon fills, slowly,
she can breathe again.
She sees me wave, recognizes my Dodge Dart,
and notices my Rollerball pen telling this story
to the dashboard writing clip.

I want to hug the place where she stands
and breathe her back to life, for God's sake.

In the long run,
the dry cleaners will close,
and the Korean family
will return to Seoul.

Two Vietnamese brothers will retrofit
the building as an investment bank
for Mekong industrialists,
and their stateside start-ups.

Factories will soon re-open in Ohio,
Connecticut, and Georgia.
In the long run,
goods will ship back to Hanoi,
as their plants are now closed.

We flattened your country, Vietnam.
We rebuilt it, so that now the mighty Mekong
can send our kids to college.

In the long run, the Mighty Mekong flows.

Slip into something comfortable.

Go easy on your self,
Release your dreams.

The copyright is yours.
This is your day.

For a limited time only.

What is the best medicine for the heart?
Someone from the help desk?
A poet in your midst?

The day begins a landslide.
It's February,
what do people do in February?
My son asks, "what does 'vivid' mean?"
He is only 8. All of us are older.

Picture a vivid February.

Charlotte snowmen

Across the street.
Around the block.
Over there.

Tell everyone:
Daylight.
Today,
on purpose.

Our neighborhood awakens to a constant urging.
Are you ready?

I'll go start the car.

The driveway poet says:
There's something that the earth does, as a planet.
It turns.
Now, we see daylight.
Now, we shift.
                      (it's your turn.)

Make believe I lived today,
surrounded by my people.
My son, chirping
in the next room.
(Yes, I am an honorable distance from
my death.)

Make believe I lived today:
How do you recognize love?
Does it draw you in?

I'm starting to see a difference in the world.
What do you see? Is it obvious?

Make believe I lived today:
I did this day for the life of me,
I gave congratulations.

Our house carries the glow to the finish.
Night was what day gave me,
Make believe I lived today.

What do you see?

I teach these words to speak,
I tell them to the line:

Peace, butter and jelly sandwich,
on artisan bread.
Imagine that, you can eat your wish,
all day long.

A Better Sandwich,
A Better World.

Sit still,
eat.

Your server will be right with you.

Peace, Butter & Jelly, Litchfield, SC

Number the days, gather the weeks.
Develop a plan, like you would in the garden.

The template says growing.
Add the soil amendments.
Dig.
Dig some more.
Observe.

Never decline a vegetable.
Stay in business.

I reach for my socks.
Tell my shoes I am coming.

There's a bowl outside
we use for the dog's food.
That bowl, yes,
that bowl.

Every morning early:
Orange juice.
The dog.
Socks and shoes.
Starbucks.

Will I ever awaken to Ethiopia
dressed as a government rebel?

Ask my cat.

Wait a minute, you rascal,
I'm trying to write this.
Stop pulling on me!

Essentially.

Essentially he is my son,
And you take care of him.
We call it the school system.

I know the solar system
and who created it,
but the school system,
who created it?

People love my son.
They learn him. They scold him.
They know him.
People.
People from the solar system,
that's who can teach.

The Stars.

Jonathan's kindergarten birthday party

Let's make a revision.

We hold the necklace:
You came in that color,
I came in this color.
We adopted you, you adopted us.

We are a family, a funny family.
55 years ago our country bombed
the country where you were born.
You weren't born yet.
Yes, that is what really happened;
what will you remember?

Can we change anything?
Will you leave our shelter?

We choose the earth.
No slippage.
I keep being your father.

Lord, don't cancel me.

I want to work.
If I can't work, I can't breathe,
and it's tough to walk.

Stay with me Lord. I mean it.
I live in Ohio now.
Please re-submit my name.
I cannot afford a plane ticket to Beijing
to look for work.

I keep trying to escape, devise
a plan to leave Sandusky.

It's ten years later.
Nothing remains of Sandusky, but you.

Treacherous,
somewhat treacherous.
And it's only Monday.

I'm going to sit here in the car
a little bit longer,
before I go inside.

A soothing Caribbean breeze
was recently introduced
at my neighborhood Trader Joe's.
It comes in three essences:
Pineapple, Coconut or Mango.

A decorative box the size of a baseball
holds the scent.
At a cost of $35, it lasts up to one month,
if you leave it open.

And you can also purchase the book
that spawned the idea,
A Marketer's Revenge by Trader Joe.

Ah, Commerce.
Ah, Winter.
How about Grapefruit and Guava?

Do you need a receipt?

Let's get married.
I make the best corn bread.
I love hiking.
I am dependable.
I am thin.

You love to read cookbooks
after dinner.
Your hair is your best part,
it will never grey.
You have written several plays.

Together, we can make things happen.
Behind our house is a creek that can flood.
Don't laugh.

Hold on to your receipt.
You love water.

Why do they bring that stuff?
You can't eat that.
There's nothing in it but pure packaging
and 100% marketing margarine.
God has bakeries hidden in Tennessee and Minnesota
that make these doodles
and a factory in South Carolina to make the fastest truck
with the biggest stick-on sign.
That truck can haul the sign and the doodles
all the way from Bangor to Boca Raton.

When it's time for my car to eat, I buy gas,
and I get a pack of doodles, maybe several,
'cause it's time for me to eat, too!

Next time you're on the highway, just for the fun of it,
bring a big plastic cake fork and dig in to the side of that gorgeous
Great Dane 18-wheeler.
God feeds America, it's big business, and it's great big trucks.

I'm so hungry all the time.
What if I learned to bake banana bread
or eat red apples with my coffee?
Please God, feed me right, something fresh.

My friend Bobby builds race cars in his mom's front yard.

For Christmas, he gave her the blue door from his '83 Camaro
to use on her Kelvinator,
and he made it fit.

They have a toaster oven in the kitchen
that's as big as a dumpster. In fact,
I think it's the glove box from his dad's '59 Cadillac Coupe,
the family car before dad and mom got divorced.

They call him 'Bobby the Wizard' at the local tech college
and his pastor says God displayed the sign of the wrench
when he was born.

I swear, the last time he washed his Ford 150,
the thing ran like a blazing chariot.

My friend Bobby.

It's already in the machine,
Press Play, and let's begin:

This remarkable day,
a thurs day.
What a gift to arrive this far in the week
unscathed, unburdened.
You are by far the biggest sapphire in the universe,
a most outstanding meteor.

Gather your wits you great human being,
and gallop forth!
Beat those Yankees!

To the degree that we know it today,
twenty years ago there was no cell phone,
no internet, no e-mail, no texting.
A boom box was larger than the biggest carry-on bag.
Today, music is packed in a wafer the size of a Pokemon card,
for no one else to hear.

So, how are we doing as a civilization?
"Are you talking to me?
I need to take this call,
just one minute, please."

When we've gone
as fast as the mind can think,
will we be able to know our friends?
What if they're only virtual ones?

I'm your teacher and I'm speaking to you.
Give me your eyes and put your fingers away
and listen.
What I'm saying is very important:
You are afraid.
You are afraid you're going to miss something.
What something?
Who are you?

Let's talk.

Eileen.

She wanted to bake a bread
that would never grow old.
She wanted to live beside it,
forever.

Some people say she never
got the flour out of her hair.
Only she knew her real age.

When you bake, it takes time.
When you live, it takes time.
Can you afford it?
Make a brioche dough
and watch it fall,
Hold on to life when it's so elastic?
Cultivate the wheat,
and the germ of the wheat?

Sourdough was her discovery,
and we thank her.
We taste the difference, Eileen.

They are your neighbors.
They love your car.
They love your landscape lighting
and the rocks.

With the amount of money they make
and the amount of money they give away,
they could take on The Water Dept.,
The Board of Ed., Parks and Rec.,
and make them all successful, simultaneously.
In Chicago, yes, Chicago.
All of the above, handled.

They shovel your walk
when you are away.
Their names: Tom and Marie.
Occupation: Very Good Neighbors.
Department: Citizens.

Digestion is a wonderful benefit of being alive.
I looked on the table today at everything to be eaten,
a huge collection of stuff: bananas, kale, spelt toast,
cups of milk and blueberry juice,
and thick pea soup with red skin potatoes.
I said, "Way to go, God!
You take all of this and make it into me.
Good job.
Thank you."

Everything I've ever done has been eaten.

We prepare, and we prepare, and we prepare,
and then it's all gone.

What makes a soup successful?
A daily dose of hope.

I'm downstairs in the kitchen,
come and find me.

I send 85 resumes daily:
- Global Gratitude Manager
- Wellness Host
- Dough Conditioner/ Pastry Chef
- Fruit Market Analyst

Yes, I lift up the seat.
No, I do not leave the seat up.

Hello?
Anybody in the market for a wonderful man?
An American Hero!

I can turn on a dime.
I am the stick that stirs your coffee.
I am diversity.
I will build you a legend.

I never complain.

I make believe it's today.

I understand.
Maybe it was the calzone.
Maybe it was the movie, the violence at the end.
Maybe it was the government's response to joblessness,
reported in the Times today, the lead article.

Maybe I don't understand.
Maybe it's okay to feel a little feeble this morning.
Heck, I'm a grown-up.

How can Sunday possibly be as challenging as a weekday?
Why is today such a tricky business?

Let me step outside now
and place my brow on the calm front lawn.
For the sake of me, I bow earthwise.
Then, I slope.

It's the hip.
It's not her bosom.
The gentle crest of our marriage.
My resting place.
Our slumber.

    until...............Thump!
The cat arrives to claim her curve,
her mother.
She is one hip cat,
              this morning.

Sing:

Lord,
Capture me.
Seize my cargo.

I am a worthy vessel,
You own me now.

Now we dream.

"Turn down the heat, will you,
it's so hot in here."

"Give me some of the blanket,
you're hoggin' all the covers."

"Don't say you know where you are,
when you don't."

"I cleaned up the kitchen last night,
so it's your turn, honey."

"If we go to New Jersey in June,
I am definitely not staying at your Mother's house."

Marriage.

Friendship/ Partnership.

Early Humans?

Leo and Florence

Celery.
Who likes Celery?
I don't mean the color,
I mean the vegetable,
the stringy kind.

What if you were part of the soup?
What if you had to lie down on a slab of bamboo
to get your hair done?
What if you had to bathe with carrots and onions?

Go ahead. Look inside the pot,
and see how deep the water is.

Go GREEN.

We're expecting a stampede of vegetarians
when we open.
Put down the gadgets, guys,
we're surrounded.

We are lost and we are found.
We are lost and we are found.
And sometimes,
We are dumbfounded.

We all need assistance:
not from the beauty parlor,
not from the lawn guy,
not from any government agency.

We need a whole lot of help,
and we can't wait.

for one moment,
for one constant moment,

I would like to hold you to my bosom
       and declare my love:

             I am your scribe.
             I am your wordsmith.

             You light my day.

What is the source of our dream?
       When do we turn away?

My duty is to write it down.

I return to the page:

The footprints are mine,
Yes, that is my scarf.

What hat will I wear today?

In the time it takes to awaken the world,
    I've decided to live.
I've decided to live like one of you.
    Be a part of me, as I'm a part of you.

I am in your midst.

This is my signature poem:

I swipe my card.
I enter my PIN.
I sign my name.

They know me.
They know it's me.
I answer "yes",
and receive the senior discount.

And then,
I shoplift the Jack Cheese.

This is how I go through my day.
This is not a translation.

You want to know how to make a
hot roast beef sandwich?

You keep a saucepan on the stove,
water ready hot,
a small basket perched on the lip.

A few slices of rare,
a few dunks in the boiling brew,
two slices of Wonder bread,
now gravy,
and you've got yourself a poem.

It's very possible:
Hearts, the size of risotto,
dance freely in my bloodstream.
They populate my arteries,
red ones and white ones.

And they make me ME,
and they make me happy

as they dance around

on this lovely day.

It was our last winter in North America.
So cold, so icy, that when you walked
you felt like you were pushing a chest of drawers
        that was about to fall on you.
A piece of me never got warm that winter and never forgot it.
Our Honda 5-speed had scars on the battery terminals
and every tire was constantly thanking the other one
when it got us there and back.
I can remember clearly what God said about the winter of '93:
"You don't have to stay in the Catskills if you don't want to.
You can move to the South, I won't mind,
but I will miss your cheeks as one blazing red freckle per side."
That voice followed us to the Carolinas
and now appears in my dogwood tree in March
as a Yellow Finch, bright as daybreak.
God owns all the geography in the world.
The weather is the rhythm that shakes the map as you unfold it.
Where do I want to live when everywhere is beautiful?
        When I awake in the morning,
the continuous rays of the sun wrap the granite porch
like fruit leather you can taste from the driveway.

Spring, the gorgeous sting of warmth!

Overheard at the Mall:

There's never anything going on for me.
He doesn't even call.

When he sees me at work,
I am another customer,
the next service point.

I want Daniel to make love to me,
but he only wants to be my manager.

I'm not in retail just to make money,
I need a man.
I want a husband.

What if he fired me?

She circles the field 3 times,
daily, at dusk.
She never minds the school kids.

A little tai chi, a little running,
a little yoga.

She is 34 years old,
the global manager of online sales
for the world's largest telecommunications company.

She is alone. She has no children, no pets.

Is she a man or a woman?

Do you know this person?

There are only 2 ways you can feel:

I feel loved.
I feel afraid.

I am either loved,
or I am afraid that I am not being loved,
or will not be loved.

There is love and there is fear,
Our summary.

Bess and David

Jonathan. Self portrait with cell phone, test tube and pencil, age nine

EPILOGUE: A Better Sandwich, A Better World.

To live in peace, to be peace, and to share peace takes incredible luck and a teacher who can guide the journey. Meditation is my teacher. I also have a meditation teacher who is a master of meditation. The sheer luck of my journey landed me in the Caribbean in 1980. I hit the jackpot in 1985 when I realized my dream as a yoga student, to live side by side with my teacher in her special abode. The ashram is a place like none other on this earth.

On my first birthday celebrated in the ashram, a close friend gifted me a card; her words would frame the exquisite experience of the next nine years.

> "What an auspicious birth, to meet a master, and what grace!
> To be able to serve her! Happy 35th Birthday, David!"

We go to movies and 3-D movies, we do extreme sports and eat extraordinary foods to see if we can go beyond the daily routine and enter a realm of constant satisfaction and contentment. "Can I be happy? Will I receive love and will I recognize it? What would it take to feel joy?" I served my teacher and I felt golden, I felt myself as stellar, as part of her greatness. My service was an example to myself and others that a spiritual path does carry redemption, that we can live in peace and thrive and be challenged. We can also overcome our differences with others. I wasn't imagining it; I was living the greatest possible encounter with a teacher of humanity, on a daily basis.

Was it all groovy? No. The path of yoga, of dedicated self-inquiry, rattles the bones. At times, I wanted to flee myself. The emotional growth I needed was formidable.

On my first day as a resident and full-time staff person, I sat for a moment in my new room; the ashramites were offering a three day chant to honor our path of yoga. I could not wait to get to the chant. Chanting is an amazing elixir; if you want to enter a state of rapture, join the chant. Remember, I had been chanting since my early days as a Bar Mitzvah student in New Jersey. Is there any difference between a rousing Hebrew verse and a Sanskrit hymn? Essentially, no. I was now chanting the name of my teacher. This special human being had blasted my heart wide open for the first time in my life just three years ago. Chanting is about devotion. You love to do it and it loves you back.

I put these words on the page, while the chant soared from the p.a. system in the courtyard. The word Shakti refers to the universal energy of Grace, the creative force.

Ashram
10/29/85

Dear Baba,

I am Exalting
I am a Child of Excitement
I have become your Heart
I have become your Shakti
I light the Sun
I am in the Guru's House
My Skin chants
My Life Blessing continues to place me
at your feet — in the most
extraordinary way you keep us
Eternal — we are beyond this world
and, here, we thrive
I know my heart is sold
Sold to my guru
He grabbed it, he stole it,
He devoured it and appointed
me his lover
I love you Baba
I love your supreme style
I love the chance you took to make
me your Brother in this dance
God Bless you, Baba
God keep you mine in Joy

daily journal, Ashram, 10/29/85

That was twenty-six years ago. I now share the vision of A Better Sandwich, A Better World. We will use food as the operating system. You must eat well to feel nourished. Keep it simple. Follow the recipes in this book. Find the force in the food that wants to feed you and build a friendship with those ingredients. Use this book as a starting point. Go and make yourself something good to eat.

It has to be a good sandwich. The bread has to be the best bread, and my choice is sprouted, flourless Ezekiel 4:9® Bread. In part, a Better World is one in which we can now find our favorite brand in a variety of supermarkets. Today, the bread does not even need flour. We can live in a Better World that is sprouted.

A Better Sandwich, A Better World. How we eat is how we feel, who we are and what we give back to our neighborhood. Good bread. Good thoughts. Good luck. People appreciate a good meal, and if it's on bread they can take it with them. A Better World. We can take our food with us and eat it at the appropriate time. What if we brought Mr. Walt Disney together with the Dalai Lama to create our next meal, our next adventure, a new humanity? For the sake of Peace, Butter and Jelly, what will it take to get you into this new, hybrid vehicle?

Every day of my life there has been enough to eat, not the case for my Grandfather. He sometimes added this tale to his story of life in Russia:

"Each week on Friday I had to go with horse and sled to purchase the food for the coming week. I visited about half a dozen merchants until I got everything we needed. On one occasion, I bought kerosene. It was late in the day and the river was already frozen over. I needed to cross the river to get home and the raft was not available. I guided the sled across the ice until the sled turned over in a remote part of the river valley. Someone helped to right the sled. I was able to travel on with nothing to eat and nothing for the horse. When I finally arrived at the house, it was nearly 11 o'clock at night. The owner's wife immediately began to holler at me, 'Why are you so late young man?' The week that followed we had the food drenched with kerosene."

My legacy distinguishes me. My family members have been writers, rebels, cooks, creators, humanitarians, and successful entrepreneurs for a century. My grandfather never dreamed that I would include his breath in a book written 100 years after he almost froze to death in a sub-zero sweat shop. 'Peace is what we are good at.' I know that he would have said that. Not peace talks, peace plans, peace initiatives or winning the peace. If sprouted grains are sufficient and we don't need flour, then how much easier can it be? Let there be peace. I can't wait. Peace, Butter & Jelly.

DESSERT

A Beginning or an Ending, It Just Depends

While waiting for the bread pudding to cool, allow me the pleasure of relating the story of Bill DeMarco. Bill and I shared many family food treats together back in the day in good old Boston.

On Wednesday, Bill DeMarco purchased a new toaster oven
as big as a carry-on suitcase.
The old one had burned itself up
when the switch to toast stayed on forever
and left a fat charcoal spot
on the blazing white kitchen back-splash.
Inside the shoe pockets of the new machine
he kept several packages of string cheese
and apricot fruit leather. Had to be apricot.
This jet-black monster oven made in Portugal
with seasonal labor from Mexico and the Marianas Islands,
was the first piece of kitchen equipment to combine food,
travel, and modern social theory.
Called the "Big One", it could toast bagels,
defrost chicken nuggets, and download
the Banana Nut Quick Bread Recipe
from *Joy of Cooking* into a 9 inch loaf pan
ready to bake, butter, and serve.

When Bill placed it in the overhead
on the morning flight to Baltimore,
none of the passengers were expecting breakfast.
While his neighbors in B and C
powered up their laptops,
he quietly extended the cable from the collapsible handle
and connected the Big One to the dataport terminal in the armrest,
aisle side,
and smoothly closed the overhead door
to conceal the connections.
The Portuguese owner's manual indicated
that using the Big One as a bread maker
was only suitable for cinnamon raisin recipes,
only once-a-week, preferably mid-week,
and on longer flights.
Charlotte to Baltimore was only 45 minutes at most,
so we would need at least two hours
at 35,000 feet if Bill was understanding
all the vowel markings in the text.

Suddenly, Captain Jim Jackson came on to announce
that a power surge in the first class cappuccino maker
would require immediate servicing
before they would be allowed to enter
the line-up for take off.
Everyone, all the passengers,
turned away from their screens
and looked at a neighbor.
"How long did the captain say, did you hear?"
Without hesitation,
Bill hit the enter key on the remote power terminal
and within 38 seconds
the warm scent of butterable bread
began to fill the forward cabin.
The Big One's data interceptor
knew that the cappuccino repair,
the line-up for take-off,
and a storm just south of Richmond
would send us via Pittsburgh
and allow us the two hours needed
for a thick crust and triple-moist interior.

When we finally landed in Baltimore,
it was declared an aviation miracle
by all the wire services.
A two-hour delay in flight 1834
had become a whole-grain celebration.
Faith and pure friendship
had turned a group of hungry travelers
away from their emergency cell phones
and closer to butter, real double churn.
A few folks at the baggage claim
had cinnamon swirled blouses
and were requesting that the arrival reps
bring more moist towels.
A lady from Nebraska en route to visit her niece
at the new culinary institute declared,
"I was a little scared when I smelled
the bread baking near the emergency exit,
but I was so grateful they finally disconnected
the cappuccino machine and let us leave.

Since I was a little girl,
I've been crazy about individual foil-top butter pats,
and that's all the crew had put on board.
Breakfast in bread, breakfast in bread!"
she exclaimed to her niece,
who was relieved to know
the headlines meant her favorite aunt
had not missed a meal in the air.

A true story?
A typical East Coast Wednesday?
Something that God made up to illustrate the future and food?

Peace, Butter and Jelly in real life?

At the end of the day,
it has nothing to do with money.
It only has to do with one thing.
That one thing is love.
The power of love.
The power of love to love you back to life
again and again.

Acknowledgements

Thank you to all the great beings and favorite places that have contributed to the creation of this book.

Jeanette and Jonathan Seidel, Deb Blevins, Terri Fritch, Peter McRae, Michelle Whitmore, Barbara Presnell, Andy Brown, Rita Ross, Judy Lynn, Rick Helms, Deborah Bosley, William Stafford, Ronald Gottesman, Peter Reinhart, Jenny Yopp and the entire staff of the Cornwell Center of Myers Park Baptist Church, Park Road Public Montessori School, Steven Lazenby, Steven Fleischer, Robert Arnold, Doug Hutto, The Theiss Family, The McClure Family, Kevin Randall, Latitude 35 Design Team, Sarah Shoemaker Roberts, The Healing Circle, UNC Charlotte, Queens University of Charlotte, Winthrop University, Central Piedmont Community College, Gardner-Webb University, Davidson College, York Technical College, Cleveland Community College, Pfeiffer University, Karen Lynden, Cathy Whatley, Chuck Hipple, Ron Wolfe, Uncle Marty Settle, South Park Swim and Tennis Club, Bing Michael, The Original Pancake House, Hank Wilson's Monday Night Men's Group, John Amen, Mary Powers, Darley Adare, Tony Abbott, Ivey Sumrell, The Public Library of Charlotte-Mecklenburg, China Bistro 88, A Sign of the Times of the Carolinas, Trader Joe's Midtown Charlotte, Litchfield Beach and Golf Resort, Florence Seidel, Richard Seidel, Leo J. Seidel, the lineage of Seidels, Saltzs and Fleischers, Toyota Motor Company, Verve Records, Lloyd McNeill, Follett Corporation and Media Resources, Eileen Grossman, and Ani Tuzman. I am also grateful to the cities of Charlotte, North Carolina; Brookline and Boston, Massachusetts; The City of New York; Union and New Brunswick, New Jersey; Sosua, The Dominican Republic.

All interior photographs were taken by Seidel family members or friends.

I apologize if I have left anyone out. You are with me always. Thank you.

Jeanette, Jonathan and David at Chimney Rock State Park, NC

Recipe Index

Savory
Butter and Yeast on Crunchy Bread 59
Exotic Quinoa Pilaf 56
La Fanega 53
Miso Soup 55
Morning Greens (Energy Soup) 59
The Concoction 49
Tortilla Mamita Casserole 65

Sweet
Best Cornbread 64
Chocolate Magico / Fruta Magica 60
Good Morning Cereal 62
Noodle Kugel 57
Peace, Butter & Jelly Chocolate Cake 63
Peach and Blueberry Cobbler 58
Rice Pudding Comfort, Holiday Style 54
TJ's Best Bread Pudding 67

Index of Poems by First Line

1964 was a quieter time 19
note of thanks 69
A soothing Caribbean breeze 90
Across the street 81
At the end of the day
Butter and the absence 14
Celery 105
Dear Baba 118
Digestion is a wonderful benefit 98
Do you need a receipt 91
Each time my wife cleans the house 32
Eileen 96
Essentially 86
Everybody on the planet 73
Everything I've ever done 99
for one moment 107
God put my Grandma on the boat 21
Hey! Look at Peter Cottontail 45
I dream 50
I got the job 75
I have taken every chance 76
I kept every precious cloud 25
I reach for my socks 85
I return to the page 108
I send 85 resumes daily 100
I teach these words to speak 83
I understand 101
I will colonize your mind 41
In the long run 78
In this new year, I hope to reach 43
Into the wagon 77
It was our last winter 112
It's already in the machine 94
It's the hip 102
It's very possible 111
Let's make a revision 87
Lord, don't cancel me 88
Make believe I lived today 82
Mr. Sommerman had a grocery 37
My father never dried his legs 38
My friend Bobby builds race cars 93
Number the days, gather the weeks 84
On Wednesday, Bill DeMarco 121
Overheard at the Mall 113
Remembering as I walk the Cape 48

She circles the field 3 times 114
She is light 12
She was born in 1935 46
Sing 103
Slip into something comfortable 79
Teaching, consulting 74
The deep peace of breakfast 33
The only technology that can serve 71
The perfect amount of words 33
The word is Love 41
There are only 2 ways you can feel 115
There were things 47
They are your neighbors 97
This is my signature poem 109
This is the vegetable hour 40
To the degree that we know it today 95
Treacherous 89
Turn down the heat, will you 104
We are lost and we are found 106
We need for the sun to shine 70
We need rain so badly 46
What is the best medicine 80
What's it like to live with Jelly 44
Why do they bring that stuff 92
Yes, I did it all 43
You don't have to read 72
You want to know 110

About the Author

David Mark Seidel is a writer, teacher, professional chef, and a successful entrepreneur with several small businesses. He trained at Boston's Restaurant Maison Robert and founded the first personal chef service, Boston's Renaissance Restaurant Man. David created the first natural foods restaurant in the Dominican Republic, the Magic Kitchen, and later the Magic Kitchen Cooking School in Charlotte, North Carolina. He also founded Casa Naima, the premier tour operation on the Dominican Republic north coast. His I.D.S. Wellness Program (Invocation, Dedication, Service) reduces health care costs by teaching individuals to maintain optimum health and reduce risk of chronic disease. A graduate of Rutgers University and trained by masters of ancient Yoga traditions, David has been a teacher of the Humanities, Culinary Arts, Yoga and Meditation for over 29 years. He has appeared on NBC-TV as a guest chef. David also taught in over 60 cities in North and South America, as well as in India, and the Caribbean. He has lectured at Queens University of Charlotte, University of North Carolina at Charlotte, Davidson College, Central Piedmont Community College and Gardner-Webb University. David lives in Charlotte with his wife of more than 32 years, Jeanette, and his son, Jonathan. To contact David: peacebutterandjelly.com and davidmarkseidel.com